Elizabeth Pomada

Places to go with children

in Northern California

with photographs by
Edward R. Susse

CHRONICLE BOOKS
870 Market Street, San Francisco

Needless to say, this book was not done by just one person. I must say "Thank you" to Julie Rosenthal, our cover girl; to Jennifer, Diana and Mark, Eric and Chris, Cindy and Christopher, and Alan, our "test" children; to Diana and John Hynds for providing a home away from home; to Don McGlinchy who has three kids of his own; to photographer Ed Susse; and to Avis, whose cars carried us over 3,996 miles in our search of Northern California. But most of all, thank you to my editor, chauffeur, idea man, hero, and the biggest child of them all — MFL.

E.P.

CONTENTS

INTRODUCTION

This book came about because Cindy and Christopher, our favorite niece and nephew, were expected to spend a summer with us — and we didn't know what to do with them. Then we thought that if we were going to do research for ourselves, we might as well do it for all our friends — and you. We explored, read books, and drove over most of Northern California, searching out places that would be educational, historical, and, as the *Pollardville Ghost Town* put it, "entertaintional." We believe that if you and your children can learn something and have fun at the same time, then the good time is worth twice as much.

We found an incredibly varied, beautiful country. And we learned the history of California at the same time. We also gave special emphasis to year-round attractions — and those that were free. We concentrated on places to go, rather than things to do, so we haven't included all the typical activities possible for youngsters in any community, like skiing, bowling, camping, hiking, family billiards, and ice skating (try the Yellow Pages). Nor have we included all the national, state, country, and city parks you would naturally know about or gravitate to. Finally, there are well-known tourist attractions that were left out because we felt they were not suitable for, or enjoyable to, children.

Special restaurants that have an appeal to youngsters, museums, steam railroads, natural wonders and man-made amusements are all here for you to try — along with a list of festivals, fairs, and feasts that have become regular annual happenings.

Local Chambers of Commerce, tourist offices, or a telephone call can give you up-to-the-minute dates, times, and prices (most attractions are privately owned and subject to changes in schedules at any time), as well as lodging information. Most places are closed on Christmas, Thanksgiving, and New Year's Day.

We know we've only scratched the surface of things to do in Northern California, and we'd like to hear about the special places you discover. In the meantime, equipped with this book and your imagination, you and your children are sure to have a wonderful time!

California Gold Country (photo by Karen Gottstein)

San Francisco – Fisherman's Wharf

8

1

SAN FRANCISCO

What is the secret of San Francisco's attraction? A combination of natural beauty, a short but lively history in which gold and disaster loom large, and a dynamic mixture of people and cultures: Spanish, Chinese, Italian, Russian, French, Japanese, and many more. Together, these elements have made a magnet that attracts visitors from all over the world.

San Francisco is a center for culture (and counterculture), business, education, entertainment, and tourism. "The City" provides a lot to see and do for children and their parents. And those formidable hills notwithstanding, the best way for a family to do it is on foot (with sweaters on hand in case of untimely winds). So pick an area and a destination, park the car or get off one of the ubiquitous bus lines, and start walking!

For openers, we suggest taking a cable car to the Fairmont Hotel on Nob Hill, and the free ride on their outside elevator to the Crown Room at the top. Night or day, the view is spectacular. From there, walk through Chinatown. Then, after a little rest or a bite to eat, walk along Upper Grant Avenue in the

North Beach area. You'll find a bustling Italian village, and crafts shops. For a 360-degree view of the Bay and The City, end up at Coit Tower on the top of Telegraph Hill. (25¢ call 362-8037 for hours.)

On the other side of town, the first 12 blocks of Clement Street is the heart of the Russian District. Nosh a piroshki, a tasty meat pastry, as you wander through the neighborhood stores. The Mission District offers Latin American groceries, a scattering of health food shops, and a multitude of Mexican delights. For kids, just as for adults, San Francisco is a fascinating town.

Hyde Street Pier – Maritime State Historic Park

Calif. Div. of Mines & Geology Mineral Exhibit and Library

Rm. 2022, Ferry Bldg., Embarcadero, foot of Market St. Tel. 557-0633. Mon.-Fri., 8 A.M.-5 P.M. Free.

● Thousands of rocks, minerals, and ore specimens fill the glass-covered displays of this impressive, well-arranged collection. Highlights include the exhibit of gold in the form of dust, ore, and nuggets and the facsimile of the enormous "Welcome Stranger" nugget. A 5-foot-high model of a quartz mill shows how gold is extracted from ore and another model shows the workings of the Idaho-Maryland gold mine. In addition to the exhibits about the official state mineral, there is a large collection of the state rock, serpentine, showing its many variations of color, texture and structure. There are also display cases for every county in the state, showing the minerals to be found in each. Maps and such intriguing literature as *A Walker's Guide to the Geology of San Francisco* (50¢) are on sale. Be sure to walk up the ramps of the Trade Center to look at the murals of life in the Pacific.

Energy Expo.

P G & E, 77 Beale. Tel. 781-4211 ext. 4248. Mon.-Fri. 9 A.M.-4:30 P.M. Free.

● Multi-media shows explaining nuclear power and planning for future energy needs. Fourteen exhibits include a saltwater aquarium showing undersea ecology, "How Electricity is Made," sources of natural gas, and more. Visitors can run a model of the first electric generators and simulate an energy dispater.

Vaillancourt Fountain

Embarcadero Plaza, foot of Market St.

● When the water in this bizarre, poured-concrete fountain is turned off, the fountain looks like an accident. But when the water is running, and you can walk over, under and around rushing falls and streams, it's wonderful. The arts and crafts fair in the Plaza during weekday lunch hours (with up to 300 craftsmen on weekends) always has lots of unusual handmade things on display.

Next door, the Hyatt Regency offers a spectacular 21st century lobby to wander around with fountain, doves in cages, a burbling brook and glass clevators that travel 20 stories.

Golden Gate Ferry

Just north of the Ferry Bldg., next to Pier 1, Embarcadero. Tel. 982-8833. Leave S.F. weekdays, about an hour and a half apart, 7:50 A.M.-8:10 P.M.; weekends, 10:25 A.M.-6:50 P.M. One-way fare: adults, 75¢; ages 6-12, 25¢.

● The Golden Gate Ferry leaves its slip at the foot of Market Street, passes the island of Alcatraz, and 30 minutes later docks in Sausalito. The shop on board serves coffee, soda and cakes (and great Bloody

Marys for parents). For many youngsters, the boat trip is the best part of their day!

Pacific Stock Exchange, Inc.

301 Pine St. Tel. 392-6533. Mon.-Fri., 8:30 A.M.-2:30 P.M. Free.

● The Pacific Coast Stock Exchange handles more buying and selling of stock than any other exchange outside of New York City. The doors open at 6:30 A.M., and from then on, the activity on the trading floor never stops. Visitors climb a flight of stairs to a glass-enclosed balcony to watch the proceedings. On one wall, four screens record every transaction on the New York, American and Pacific Coast exchanges. The fourth screen flashes the latest financial news which could affect stock prices. Once upstairs, you can push a button for a recording that explains everything going on below.

Museum of Money of the American West

The Bank of California, 400 California St., downstairs. Tel. 765-0400. Banking days, 10 A.M.-3 P.M. Free.

● This small but beautifully mounted collection of gold and other historical mementos provides intriguing glimpses of banking and mining in the Old West. Privately minted coins from Utah, Colorado, and California illustrate the kind of money used before the U.S. Mint

was established in San Francisco. Shiny counterfeit coins, and counterfeit detectors as well, are also on display. One method, serious enough to be dubbed "the platinum menace," was to hollow coins and fill them with platinum, which was then worth much less than gold. A 19th-century engraving shows the activities at the Comstock Lode, a Nevada mine, which produced over $300,000,000 in gold and silver used to finance the Union during the Civil War. Be sure to read the amusing note about William C. Ralston, one of early San Francisco's leading financiers, who led a quiet raid on the U.S. Sub-Treasury so he could exchange gold bars for coin to prevent a run on his bank.

A World of Oil

Standard Oil of California, 555 Market St. Tel. 894-4895. Mon.-Fri., 9 A.M.-4 P.M. Tours of building (by appt.) any weekday, 9:30 A.M.-4 P.M.

● Standard Oil of California presents a show and exhibit telling how oil is found, produced, and used for energy, heat, lubrication and a multitude of products we couldn't live without. The multi-media program starts with a short film showing how tremendous amounts of time and underground pressure change decayed plants and animals into petroleum and how oil was obtained and used in the past. The search and uses for black gold are illustrated with photographs, models of rigs, actual drilling tools and a mural of a modern refining plant. Three life-size dioramas show the role oil has played in American life. One with particular appeal for children portrays a family in a 1910 kitchen.

McGoon's Magic Cellar

630 Clay St. Tel. 986-1433. Tues.-Sat., 8 P.M.-2 A.M. $2 cover charge and two-drink minimum per person (soft drink o.k.).

● McGoon's Magic Cellar houses an amazing collection of magic tricks, magicians' memorabilia and even a few wandering magicians. Houdini's chains and letters are here, as are shadow boxes, spirit cabinets, a basket with swords through it and levitation couches. Thirty tons of costumes and equipment owned by the late Carter the Great and found by accident in a San Francisco garage make up the basis of this everchanging collection. There are magic shows on the hour, and there is a special section for teenagers who are over 16. Sandwiches and meals are available. McGoon's is basically a saloon, but children are allowed.

Levi Strauss History Room

2 Embarcadero Center. Tel. 391-6200. Mon.-Fri., 10 A.M.-4 P.M. Free.

● Memorabilia of "the pants that won the West." Photos of Levi's customers: the loggers, goldminers, cowboys, and railroad workers — and a display of original canvas and denim Levis will fascinate any jeans' wearer.

Exhibit at A World of Oil

Wells Fargo History Room

420 Montgomery St. Tel. 396-2648.
Banking days, 10 A.M.-3 P.M. Free.

● A Wells Fargo Concord Stagecoach is the centerpiece of this history of Wells Fargo and the Old West. Treasure boxes and old money, iron doors from the Wells Fargo building in the old gold-country town of Chinese Camp, "The Pioneers' Ten Commandments," 60 samples of California gold, a map of Black Bart's 28 stagecoach robberies and many other items provide sidelights of Western history. Early photography methods are on display, with sample photographs and cameras, and the high seat and iron headrest used for daguerrotypes. There's even a Buffalo Bill collection. Stamp collectors will want to spend time with the huge collection of stamps and postmarks of early California towns.

Marrakech Restaurant

419 O'Farrell St. Tel. 776-3600.
Weekdays, 6-11 P.M. (kitchen closes
at 10); Fri. and Sat., dinner served at
7 and 9 P.M. Expensive. Reservations
advised.

● Walk into Marrakech and you walk into Morocco — white-washed walls, colorful tiles, airy trellises that make patterns on the ceiling and silken pillows to lounge on before low brass tables. Marrakech is high-priced, but it's an experience you and your children will never forget. Once you are seated, you wash your hands with rose water poured from a golden samovar and you're given a long bath towel to use as a napkin. The first course is a delicious vinegary salad of tomatoes, eggplant and other vegetables all mashed together. You use warm Algerian bread as a scoop, or just your fingers; silverware is taboo. Then comes Basteleh — pigeon pie with sugar and cinnamon. Then delicate lemon chicken. Then sumptuous lamb, dripping with honey and almonds. Then couscous fassi, my favorite, a wheat and chickpea stew that you roll into balls and pop into your mouth. Then collapse, rest, recline, relax. A girl in native costume brings water for your hands again and sprays you with orange flower water. A huge plate of dates, bananas, figs, grapes and other fruits in season is served with hot sweet mint tea in gold filigree glasses. (Our 12-year-old insisted that we peel him a grape!) Marrakech is a wondrous experience that will make any evening a special occasion.

Lyle Tuttle's Tattoo Museum

30 7th Street. Tel. 864-9798. Mon.,
Wed. & Fri. noon-4 P.M. $1.

● Thousands of tattoos, designs and instruments, including a Bear War (1898) tattoo pattern and pre-Columbian devices, make this one of the most unique museums in the world.

The Asawa Fountain

Hyatt Hotel on Union Square (Stockton between Sutter & Post)

● Ruth Asawa, creator of the Mermaid Fountain in Ghirardelli Square, has given the people of San Francisco a one-stop tour of the people and places that make up The City. This round (14' diameter) fountain, on the step's of the hotel's plaza, was molded in bread dough — the same dough children use for sculpture — and cast in bronze. And the little people, trees, Chinese dragon, gingerbread houses, and school buses demand to be touched. If you stand at the bottom of the fountain you'll face the Ferry Building; then as you go around the fountain counter-clockwise, you'll see Coit Tower, Broadway, Maritime State Park, the Cannery, the Zoo, the Mission District — everything laid out in the same general direction as it is in real life. A group of Noe Valley schoolchildren created one of the fountain's forty-one plaques to depict the children of San Francisco. Your children will enjoy figuring out which one it is.

Victoria Station Restaurant

Embarcadero at Broadway. Tel. 433-4400. Mon.-Fri., 11:30 A.M.-2:30 P.M., 5:30-11 P.M. Fri. and Sat.; 5 P.M.-midnight.

● A fascinating complex of dining rooms made up of old railroad cars form this unique steak and prime rib restaurant. Authentic railroad furnishings and memorabilia from England create an atmosphere especially entertaining for kids. Platform 1 is the free baggage-cart salad bar where you make your own salad out of tasty fresh ingredients. Platform 2 is beef: about $3 for lunch, $5.45-$8 for dinner. Shrimp Victoria, sauteed in wine and garlic sauce, is the only non-beef dish on the menu. This is a blossoming chain with new restaurants popping up all over. At Platform 3, sauteed mushrooms served in sizzling skillets, and Platform 4 is dessert — chocolate bavarian creme pie.

Chinatown Wax Museum

601 Grant Ave. Tel. 392-1011. Daily, 10 A.M.-11 P.M. School group discounts. Adults, $1.50; ages 6-12, $1.00.

● The Chinese Wax Museum, unique in the United States, presents 31 authentic-looking scenes capturing the history, traditions, customs and pageantry of China and San Francisco's Chinatown. You find Marco Polo meeting Kublai Khan, a classic Chinese opera frozen in mid-song, a traditional Chinese wedding, a dinner for immigrant Chinese on board a Gold Rush ship, and a court lady's boudoir. The music changes from scene to scene. The Chinese New Year parade and celebration dragon are also here. There is one aisle of burial and torture scenes that I do *NOT* recommend for children, but it can be easily circumvented if the watchful parent moves directly from the grocery-store to the herb shop. Actually, the herb shop is particularly timely — acupuncture charts and needles are prominently displayed.

Golden Gate Fortune Cookie Co.

23 Ross Alley (above Grant, bet. Washington and Jackson Sts.). Tel. 781-3956. Mon.-Sat., 9 A.M.-8 P.M. Free.

● You can stand in the doors of the bustling factories in Ross Alley and see just how fortune cookies are made. You and your children may prefer not to know; it's not a very romantic process. A row of tiny griddles revolves under a hose that squirts dough onto each pan. The pans continue their circle, cooking the dough on their way to the fortune-cookie maker. He picks up the browned wafer, pushes it onto a spur to give it the first fold, inserts the paper fortune, presses the final fold, and puts the cookie into a muffin tin to harden.

Lane Hueng Fortune Cookie Factory

1507 Grant. Tel. 982-9723. Mon.-Sat., 9 A.M.-8 P.M. Free tours by appt.

● Small families are welcome to poke their heads through the door to see the cookie makers and smell the good smells, whenever they're in the neighborhood. For a large

group of visitors, it's best to call before arriving.

● *DIM SUM* — also called Chinese tea or Chinese breakfast and, translated, "heart's delights" — is one of the nicest ways I know of to start a Saturday or Sunday. *Dim sum* is simply little bites of good things. A waitress or waiter comes around with a huge tray, from which you choose small plates of such delicacies as steamed pork buns, curry cakes, beef dumplings, shrimp rolls, etc. Two of our favorite San Francisco *dim sum* restaurants are:

Dragon Fountain Restaurant

941 Kearny. Tel. 362-8299. Daily ex. Wed., 7 A.M.-4 P.M.

● Dragon Fountain is a small, friendly, quiet Chinese tea house. *Dim sum* is 60¢ a plate (your final bill is calculated by the number of plates on your table) and quite tasty. The spare ribs in black bean sauce is very good, and the cold coconut cream for dessert is special.

Yank Sing Restaurant

671 Broadway. Tel. 781-1111. Daily, 10 A.M.-5 P.M.

● Yank Sing is one of the most popular restaurants in town. On weekends the lines waiting for seats are long. The *dim sum* is plentiful, delicious, and varied. We find something new to taste on each visit. Big parties are seated around lazy susan tables, so that everyone can reach out for his share. A tab of $18 for six people is standard. Remember that you pay for the number of plates on your table. So if a dish like steamed shrimps comes on two plates, and there are just two or three of you eating, ask for just half the order. That way, you can have three shrimps to taste and still have room for more "heart's delights."

Chinese Historical Society of America

17 Adler Place (bet. Grant and Columbus, just south of Broadway). Tues.-Sun., 1-5 P.M. Free.

● Chinese societies throughout California have contributed to the fascinating collection in this small, almost hidden museum. Household and religious items, private and official papers, photographs and a variety of 19th-century artifacts tell us how the Chinese lived in and contributed to the development of California. An altar block and a printing block from the Napa Chinese Temple are on display, as is an elaborate ceremonial sword from the Hanford Taoist Temple. You'll also see porcelain pillows, Buddhist leaflets, 19th-century clothes from both the highborn and laborers, opium pipes, vases and bottles, gold-mining and railroading lore and photographs and documents from the earthquake. To find Adler Place, stay on the south side of Grant Avenue and look for a catty-corner street between Pacific and Broadway.

T'ien Hou Miao Temple

125 Waverly Place, 4th fl. 10 A.M.-5 P.M. & 7-9 P.M. Daily.

● A ceiling teaming with wood carved mythological personages, shelters a gold altar for the goddess of the temple and other smaller altars around the room. 25¢ will bring you advice from shaken joss sticks, and perhaps a spot of tea, in this last functioning joss house in town.

The Old Mint

88 Fifth St. Tel. 556-3630. Tues.-Sun. 10 A.M.-4 P.M. Free.

● Built to withstand fire and earthquakes, this restored mint is now a museum housing restored rooms, a Victorian toy town display, pioneer money, a modern computer terminal and a million dollar gold bar collection. The clock in the "superintendent's office" reads "Time is Money." Other forms of money, such as tokens, notes, and walrus and seal skins are on display. Visitors can strike their own souvenir medal on an 1869 coin press.

Cable Car Museum

Corner of Washington and Mason Sts. Tel. 474-1887. Free.

● All three cable car lines in San Francisco are run by the huge revolving red and yellow wheels in the Cable Car Barn. Visitors can watch the wheels from a gallery, where there are samples of the cable itself and charts explaining how the cable cars work. You can see a photographic history of the cable cars and an exhibit of three old cars, including the first one to operate in San Francisco (in 1873). It might be a good idea to combine the Car Museum visit with a cable car ride, since the visit can answer many of the questions the children will ask about the workings of this cheerful San Francisco tradition.

Pioneer Hall, Society of California Pioneers

456 McAllister St. Tel. 861-5278. Mon.-Fri., 10 A.M.-4 P.M. Free (children under 16 must be with adult).

• Photos of the 1906 San Francisco earthquake and fire and the 1915 Exposition fill rack upon rack in this long room. There is also a free slide show about the earthquake. Wall cases show artifacts of the gold miners, photos of the construction of the transcontinental railroad, including one of the driving of the Golden Spike and a fantastic menu used in an early railroad dining car. Fire trumpets, an old stagecoach, a model of the Napa County grist mill, a model ship and varied furnishings of the San Francisco pioneers are among the other interesting items on display.

San Francisco Museum of Art

Veterans Memorial Bldg., Van Ness at McAllister. Tel. 863-8800. Tues.-Fri., 10 A.M.-10 P.M. Sat. and Sun., 10 A.M.-5 P.M. Free.

• Across the street from the City Hall (you might like to walk through the Visitors Center, a changing mini-museum of S.F. history where you can buy a Cable Car medal or other historical memorabilia. 558-2525; M-F, 8:30-4:30, Free) is the San Francisco Museum of Art, a constantly changing exhibit of modern art, from photography and paintings to sculpture, architecture, design and graphic art. The Sunday paper will alert you to the latest show. The Museum has a very active film program, with special programs for children throughout the year. Classics like "The Red Balloon" are shown at a nominal charge.

On the ground floor of the building, left of the entrance, is the American Legion Trophy Room (not connected with the Museum). This is a collection of crusaders' swords, pirates' cutlasses, flintlocks and carbines, General Pershing's West Point shako and various weapons and medals. Ask the guard for the key to get in and out. (Free.)

Haas-Lilienthal House

2007 Franklin. Tel. 441-3004. Wed. 1-3:30 P.M. Sat. & Sun. 12:30-4:30, Adults, $1; students and seniors 50¢.

• This gorgeous Queen Anne Victorian, built in 1886, is a completely furnished memory of yesteryear. There's even a cat snoozing on the dining room sofa!

Shandygaff Restaurant

1760 Polk St. Tel. 441-1760. Tues.-Sat., 11:30 A.M.-10 P.M.; Sun., 4:30-10 P.M.

● The best peanut butter sandwich in the world lives at Shandygaff. It's hearty nut butter, thick slices of banana, and huge drips of honey on thickly sliced homemade wheat bread — too big to put your mouth around (1.75) and sometimes too much to finish at one time. There are salads, other sandwiches like avocado, tomato, and alfalfa sprouts, and "Specials of the day." Entrees average $5 and pots of soy butter and sweet butter with baskets of delicious, hearty bread come with everything. Hanging greenery enhances this natural foods restaurant where everything really tastes good.

Hippo Hamburgers

2025 Van Ness Ave. Tel. 771-3939. Daily, 11 A.M.-3:30 A.M.

● There are 57 kinds of hamburgers to choose from in this cheerful, circus-like restaurant. There are Italian burgers, onionburgers, Hawaiian burgers, Tahitian burgers and Cannibalburgers at prices ranging from $2-$3.50, all served as rare as you like. The adventurous might try the "nudeburger" — a roll-less hamburger smothered in ice cream, hot fudge, chopped nuts, a cherry, and a pickle. The children's menu offers giraffeburgers, rhinoburgers, and gorrillaburgers, ($1.30). Sandwiches and good desserts, such as warm banana fritters with hot cinnamon sauce, round out the menu. Hippo bibs and lollipops and balloons are there for the asking, and birthday boys and girls will be energetically sung to.

Octagon House

2645 Gough St. Tel. 885-9796. 1st Sun., 2nd and 4th Thurs. of month, 1-4 P.M. Free.

● This lovely and unusual eight-sided home is the headquarters of the Colonial Dames of America residence in California, as well as a gracious museum of Americana. Knowledgeable docents will take as much time as you wish to tell you about the house and its furnishings. Look for the pack of Revolutionary-era playing cards (with soldiers and Indians on the backs) and a Queen Anne's chest (1727) with a secret drawer. The 13-star flag, dishes taken from an English ship by the U.S.S. Constitution in the

Shandygaff Restaurant

War of 1812, the 19th-century rocking settee (a "mammy bench"), make the Octagon House a pleasant and educational stop during a walk on Union Street.

While browsing on Union Street, be sure to stop at Urban Antiques (1861 Union, tel. 931-7063) to hear marvelous music boxes and nickelodeons.

Japan Cultural Center

Post and Buchanan Sts. Tel. 346-3242/922-6776.

• On Sunday afternoons, the Peace Plaza, with its reflecting pools and five-tiered Peace Pagoda, is the center of many entertaining happenings, such as music and dance programs and judo, karate, and kendo (fencing) matches. You can fish for an oyster with a pearl in it. On other days, your children might like to wander through the goldfish, bonsai, paper, grocery, gift, and book stores in this cultural complex. The streets nearby offer interesting Japanese hardware and gift stores and restaurants. Samurai movies and theatrical programs that will attract older children are scheduled nearby.

Suehiro Restaurant

1737 Post St. Tel. 922-6400. Mon.-Sat., 11:30 A.M.-2:30 P.M., 6-9:45 P.M.; Sun. 12:30-9 P.M. Closed Tues.

• Suehiro, in the Japan Center, is a classic Japanese restaurant with a name that is well known and popular in Japan as well as San Francisco.

You may sit Japanese-style or western-style in private rooms or in the handsome main dining room. Luncheon is reasonable — from $2 for noodles in a tasty broth with egg or bean cake, — the "Special of the Day," $2.25 for a teriyaki burger, $3.50 for assorted raw fish, $4.50 for sukiyaki and *shabu shabu,* a meal of beef and vegetables boiled in a special sauce at your table. You might also try *donburi,* or "meal in a bowl." Dinners are higher priced and more varied, but they, too, are served with grace and charm by kimono-clad waitresses.

Ghirardelli Chocolate Manufactory

Ghirardelli Square, North Point and Larkin Sts. Tel. 776-5500. Daily, 11:30 A.M.-10 P.M.; Fri. and Sat. to midnight.

• Since the beginning of the century, Ghirardelli Stone-ground

Festival in Japantown

Chocolate has been a popular trade name throughout the West. This red brick, aromatic ice cream and candy shop invokes that name in a nostalgic corner of the old Ghirardelli factory. After filling out an order form and paying the cashier, you locate a marble-topped table in the crowded room or on the sunny patio in front. Hold on to your table, taking turns watching the chocolate-making machinery in the back of the room until your order number is called. Bonanza Sundaes are $1.45, the "Twin Peaks" (chocolate and vanilla ice cream under marshmallow and chocolate sauce with whipped cream fog) is $1.55 and the Golden Gate Banana Split is $1.85. The best buy may be the hot chocolate (75¢), a large mug of ambrosial chocolate topped with dozens of tiny melting marshmallows.

Ghirardelli Square, in the block bounded by North Point, Polk, Beach and Larkin Sts., is a nice place to spend an afternoon. In this charmingly restored complex of Victorian buildings, you can browse through Japanese, Dutch, Finnish, Mexican, Greek and American stores; relax around a delightful mermaid fountain; hear strolling string quartets; delight in a kite store; eat a sandwich or a meal in a Mexican, Mandarin, Hungarian or Italian restaurant, all with wonderful views of the bay.

San Francisco Experience

333 Jefferson St., Fisherman's Wharf. Tel. 474-7272. Daily performances every 45 minutes from 11:15 A.M.-9 P.M. Sun.-Thurs.; to 11:15 P.M. Fri. & Sat. Adults, $1.75; children, $1.

● This multimedia show uses 30 computerized projectors, a curving 180-degree screen and a wondrous array of lights, music, narration and sound effects to bring you the past and present of San Francisco. Foghorns and the ocean lapping at your feet transport you back to San Francisco's beginnings — the romantic days of the gold rush, the terrifying fire and earthquake. Then you review the peoples and buildings, restaurants and nightclubs, shows and songs that make up today's exciting city. Once again you hear the quiet sounds of he ocean — and 40 exciting minutes have gone by before you know it.

San Francisco Maritime Museum

Foot of Polk St. (at Beach St.) Tel. 673-0700. Daily, 10 A.M.-5 P.M. Free during Oct.-May; $1 adults; 50¢ ages 7-17; 25¢ school groups during June-Sept.

● The Maritime Museum is a mecca for ship lovers of all ages. The maritime history of San Francisco, clippers, down-Easters, British iron ships, schooners, etc., are here in models, photos, figureheads, tools and tackle. Barkentines, cutters, cod fishers, the bark Kenilworth, the H.M.S. Bounty, guns and harpoons, scrimshaw, diaries and ships' logs are just some of the things on the upstairs level. A model of Mare Island in 1870 and the ferry exhibit are of special interest. The 19-foot sloop "Mermaid," which one man sailed from Osaka to San Francisco in three months, rests outside. Billy Bones, Blackbeard, Mary Read and Anne Bonny are some of the pirates standing at the entrance to the Steamship Room. Inside, you'll find models of the Queen Mary, and various cargo and warships from World War I to the present.

San Francisco Maritime State Historic Park

Foot of Hyde St. Tel. 776-2272. Daily, 10 A.M.-6 P.M. Adults, 75¢; ages 6-17, 25¢.

● Climb aboard a sailing lumbership, a steam schooner and the last paddle-wheel ferry to operate on San Francisco Bay. New plastic wands tell you about the ships, with narrations dramatized by sounds of creaking timbers, whistles and the cries of seagulls. The *C.A. Thayer* is a typical West Coast lumber schooner that operated as a salmon packet and then a codfisher. You can go below decks to see how the crew lived, check the captain's cabin and the galley and get behind the wheel. *The Wapama* is a bigger ship with noticeably less roll and sway at anchor. Visitors descend the art nouveau curving staircase to the dining room, peek into the quarters of the seamen and at the closet-sized "honeymoon suite." The *Eureka*, the last of the paddle-wheel ferries, features a display of dozens of antique cars and trucks on her lower deck. Upstairs, there's a newstand stocked with all of the

1920 magazines and candies. Our favorite thing is the old nickelodeon. For 25¢ you can dance through the cavernous, empty vessel to the tunes of yesteryear. On the pier, old signs, lifeboats, fire wagons, the stern wheel of the riverboat *Petaluma* and an assayer's office tell their stories. And the ship's store at the entrance to the state park shows you what today's seamen use on board. *Hercules,* a 1907 ocean-going steam tug, and *Alma,* last of the S.F. Bay schooners are new additions.

The Wine Museum of San Francisco

633 Beach. Tel. 673-6990. Tues.-Sun. 11 A.M.-5 P.M.; Sun. noon-5 P.M. Free. Children must be accompanied by adults.

● The story of wine in art, quotable quotes, sculpture, history and mythology is nicely laid out for comfortable browsing. The Franz W. Sichel glass collection in back in-

San Francisco Maritime Museum

cludes glasses dating back to Roman times. There's even one said to be used by Queen Elizabeth I.

Old Brittany Restaurant

The Cannery, 2801 Leavenworth St. Tel. 776-6996. Daily ex. Tues., 11 A.M.-9 P.M.; Fri. and Sat., to 11 P.M.

● The old Brittany offers 50 varieties of crepes, large thin pancakes filled with you-name-it and folded into a square. Eggs, sausage, & cheese, blue cheese & apples ($2.25), and snails in garlic butter are our choices. If you're hungry enough, start your meal with the best French onion soup in town, a traditional delight covered with melted cheese. For dessert, try Wil Wright's delicious ice cream — the Nesselrode Bula, made with chestnuts, fruits, rum and brandy is super.

The Cannery, at Fisherman's Wharf in the block bounded by Jefferson, Leavenworth and Beach Sts., is an old fish cannery, remodeled into a beautiful complex of art galleries, book shops, clothing, furniture, jewelry and gift stores, a movie theatre, a gourmet food shop and delicatessen, and French, English, Mexican, American and Chinese restaurants. Street musicians and a glass elevator in the courtyard, the Mexican and African art shops inside the complex are our youngsters' favorite things here.

Wharf Wax Life Museum

275 Jefferson St. Tel. 776-6427.

Sun.-Thurs., 10 A.M.-10 P.M.; Fri. and Sat., to 12 P.M. Adults, $1.50; ages 5-12, 75¢.

● There's something here for every age group. Cast and costumed in 27 exhibits are a galaxy of 100 figures from the worlds of history, literature and religion. The Tin Man, Hansel & Gretel, and Rip Van Winkle represent the fairytale kingdom; Frankenstein and Dracula will please the young horror fans. Emperor Norton and the Barbary Coast recapture San Francisco's past, while a Haight-Ashbury scene and Jackie and Onassis immortalize the present.

Ripley's Believe It or Not! Museum

175 Jefferson St. Tel. 771-6188. Daily, 9 A.M.-11 P.M. summer; 10 A.M.-10 P.M. winter; later on weekends. Adults, $2.50; under 12, $1.25.

● Over 2,000 oddities and puzzles are displayed along the Crooked Lane that leads you through this amusing collection. You can study such curiosities as Jesse James' first gun, the world's smallest violin, Mother Goose, a two-headed goat, a log cabin made of 16,360 Lincoln pennies and, if your eyes and faith are strong enough, a display of "fully dressed" fleas. The children will want to spend hours here.

Museum of Witchcraft & Magic

235 Jefferson. Tel. 673-9765. Winter:

11 A.M.-10 P.M. Mon.-Thu.; Fri. & Sat. til midnight. Summer: 9 A.M.-11 P.M. Mon.-Thur.; Fri. & Sat. til midnight. Adults, $2.50; children, $1.25.

● Almost 2,000 artifacts of magical practices, from primitive times to the present, have been assembled in this eerie collection. Voodoo dolls, crystal balls, the world's largest hologram, alchemist ingredients from 75 countries, Haitian voodoo drums and an Egyptian scarab are all here.

Wax Museum at Fisherman's Wharf

145 Jefferson St. Tel. 885-4834. Daily, 9 A.M.-12 P.M., summer; 10 A.M.-10 P.M., winters; later on weekends. Adults, $2.50; ages 6-12, $1.25.

● Princess Grace and Prince Rainier, Queen Elizabeth and Prince Phillip, and Emperor Hirohito pay court to the visitor in this interesting museum. America's musicians and artists sit for a group portrait, as do such movie stars as Chaplin, Dietrich, Wayne, and Cooper. Elizabeth Taylor confronts all five husbands. Alice steps through the rabbit hole. In the San Francisco section, John Sutter drinks in an 1848 San Francisco saloon, while Emperor Norton broods in the corner. The Chamber of Horrors is horrible, but carefully marked so you can't wander in unintentionally. The Hall of Religions is very impressive.

Enchanted World of San Francisco

Jefferson and Mason Sts. Tel. 441-6262. Daily, 9 A.M.-midnight, summer; 10 A.M.-10 P.M., winter. Adults, $1.25; ages 6-13, 65¢.

● Follow the red brick road to the pretty pink cable car and ride through San Francisco's history. Disneyesque animated characters sing to you as you travel through the Gold Rush days to the building of the city in 1855 and its multitude of international villages — Polish grocers, Russians, Little Italy, the Latin Quarter and the Chinese New Year. When you hit the Barbary Coast, you're warned to hold on to your wallet and your life. The 1906 fire and earthquake threaten to engulf your car. Finally, you come to the rebuilding of the city, the elegant Pan-Pacific Exposition and fireworks! Younger children will really enjoy this.

The Balclutha

Pier 43, Embarcadero (foot of Powell St.). Tel. 776-1175. Daily, 9 A.M.-10:30 P.M. Adults, $1.50; 13-18, 75¢, ages 6-12, 25¢.

● This floating museum tells visitors all about shipping in San Francisco during the Gold Rush. One of the last surviving square-rigged Cape Horners, the Balclutha once flew 25 sails in its 17 trips around the Horn. Kids can spin the wheel, visit the "slop chest" and galley and look at the skipper's red plush settee and

The Golden Hinde II at Fisherman's Wharf

the trunks of belongings and mementos that reveal how the sailors lived. Be sure to read the sea chanties and rousing tales of Barbary Coast dance halls and windjammers. Below decks is a complete model of a salmon cannery.

The Golden Hinde

Pier 41, Fisherman's Wharf. Tel. 392-4880 Daily 10-6; Adults $2, children $1.50; school groups 50¢.

• This replica of Sir Francis Drake's famed ship traveled from England to celebrate Drake's discovery of the Bay Area. Visitors soon find themselves lost among memories of Drake, his merry men and their exciting, gold-hungry Queen, Elizabeth. The cannon, furnishings, sails and rigging are as authentic as possible. The only thing missing is the crew.

Alcatraz Island

Pier 43½, Fisherman's Wharf. Tel. 398-1141. 9 A.M.-3 P.M., tours every half hour by reservation only. Adults $2; children $1.

• Wear walking shoes and bring a sweater on this educational, fascinating-yet-depressing visit. Tours last 2½ hours.

Bay Cruise

Pier 43½, Fisherman's Wharf. Tel. 398-1141. Tours from 10 A.M.-4 P.M. Adults, $3.25; ages 11-17, $2.25; ages 5-11, $1.25; under 5, free.

• On a sunny day in San Francisco, there's nothing nicer for all of the family than the 75-minute cruise on San Francisco Bay. The guide points out the special sites and buildings and tells their history. The information is enlightening, but the really important thing is the passage around that beautiful bay.

Tiburon & Angel Island Ferries

Harbor Tours, Inc., Pier 43½, Fisherman's Wharf. Tel. 398-1141. Leaves S.F. to Tiburon and Angel Island: 10, 12, 2, 3:45, (5:30 in summer). In winter, weekends and holidays only. Roundtrip, Tiburon: adults and children, $2. Angel Island: adults, $2.25; under 12, $1.25.

• The Red & White Fleet crosses the bay from Fisherman's Wharf to the romantic inlet at Angel Island to the little town of Tiburon. A snack bar is available, but most people spend the hour on board (40 minutes to Angel Island) staring at the bay, and the seagulls that seem to follow you. For description of Angel Island, see p. 38. A helicopter (Commodore Air Tours circles Alcatraz in 4 minutes, $6, adults; $2, children) also docks at Pier 43. There is a weekend ferry service between Berkeley and Tiburon via Angel Island.

Cost Plus

2552 Taylor St. Tel. 673-8400. Mon.-Sat. 10 A.M.-9 P.M. Sun. 11-7.

• Three huge crowded stores and a

garden nursery offer many hours of browsing contentment. The main building offers a wide variety of baubles and bangles. There are cooking pots, candles, carved boxes, an extensive array of chinaware, straw baskets, bedspreads, toys, trinkets, jewelry, ethnic clothes and exotic foods from India, Italy, Japan, Mexico, Korea, China, Greece, Israel — and just about everywhere else. Across the street, the furniture store stocks colorful rugs from India, furniture from Mexico and wickerware galore. The Arts and Antiques building houses an extensive gem and mineral collection, along with interesting old posters, jewelry, Russian figurines and statuary from Thailand and the Philippines. People on their way to the Orient stop here first to check prices and availability of treasures.

S.F. Fire Dept.
Pioneer Memorial Museum

655 Presidio Ave. Tel. 861-8000. Daily, 1-5 P.M., and by appt. Free.

● Ring the bell at the side of the building and a smiling fireman welcomes you to "his" museum. On-duty firemen take turns keeping shop. Awe-inspiring photos of today's fire fighters mingle with uniforms, bells, trophies and mementos of men and machines, the silver speaking trumpet, leather buckets, buffalo-leather fire hose and other mementos of yesteryear. Lillie Coit, the darling of the S.F. Fire Dept., has her own case of remembrances. A 1912 fire chief's buggy,

an Ahrens-Fox Piston Pumper and an 1890 American LaFrance Steam Fire Engine (the department still uses only American LaFrance engines) fill the center of the room. Just as we were all getting really involved in the exhibit, the alarm rang and our guide had to leave for a fire. We all ran out of the room, slam-locked the door and waved as the firemen sped off to another battle.

California Historical Society

2090 Jackson St. Tel. 567-1848. Wed. & Sat., 10 A.M.-4 P.M., Sun. 1-5 P.M. Adults $1; students & senior citizens 50¢; 1st Saturday of the month, free. Tours at 1:30.

● The former Whittier Mansion is now a memorial to the San Francisco Academy of Art and to California artists. It features revolving exhibits of California art. En route to the second floor exhibit, you pass through the gracious Whittier drawing rooms, with their beautiful parquetry, handsome fireplaces, carved wainscotting. Up curving staircases the sketches, diaries and finished works of the first San Francisco artists are usually on display.

Museum of Russian Culture

2450 Sutter St. Tel. 921-7631. Sat. 1-3, or by appt. Free.

● A visit to this small museum will provide children with a colorful introduction to Russian culture. There are photographs, paintings, letters, medals and silks from the families of the Czars — including some funny photos of Anastasia and her sisters. The great writers, musicians, dancers and artists of Russia are remembered in portraits, autographs, first editions and memorabilia. Pushkin, Tolstoy, Pavlova and Nureyev line the walls. Scientific achievements are also exhibited. The photos and models of Fort Ross are especially interesting. Our youngster spent a long time poring through the scrapbooks of money. Although there aren't enough labels for a self-guided tour, kindly old Nick Mashe, the museum's curator, delights in telling you all about the collection.

San Francisco African-American Historical and Cultural Society

680 McAllister St. Tel. 864-1010. Tues.-Sat. 1-5. Free.

● African and Black American artists and inventors are honored in the exhibit hall of this cultural society. Clothing, pottery, historical documents and crafts are displayed, and a library is open to students of Afro-American history. The exhibit of George Washington Carver's many uses of the peanut is a wonder, and the exhibit on the Black West drew all the young cowboys. San Francisco author Ernest Gaines (*The Autobiography of Miss Jane Pittman and Long Day in November*) frequently gives talks and readings for young people at the society.

Mission San Francisco de Asis (Mission Dolores)

16th & Dolores. Tel. 621-8203. Summer: 9:30 A.M.-4:30 P.M.; Winter: 10-4. 25¢ donation.

● Built in 1776, the mission is San Francisco's oldest structure. The unique Corinthian and Moorish architecture is not at all like other California missions. We liked the cemetery best.

Avenue Photoplay Society

Avenue Theatre, 2650 San Bruno Ave. (Silver Ave. turnoff from Bayshore Freeway). Tel. 486-2636. Fri., 8 P.M.

● The Avenue Photoplay Society is a group of film and theatre-organ buffs who, some years back, imported what is now the largest Wurlitzer theatre pipe organ in the West. On Friday nights they use the organ to accompany the great silent films of Chaplin, Keaton, Griffith and others. The program begins with an organ concert by such fine local musicians as Bob Vaughn, who played for the silents the first time they came around. The movie starts at 8:30. On a quiet night, ask someone to give you a tour of the enormous pipes and bellows that give the organ its umph.

Josephine D. Randall Junior Museum

199 Museum Way at Roosevelt (upper Market St. area, up Fifteenth

St. west of Castro). Tel. 863-1399. Tues.-Sat., 10 A.M.-5:30 P.M.; Sun., noon-5 P.M. Free.

● High on a sunny hill overlooking the city, this museum and zoo is especially designed for children. Here they can watch a seismograph, see dinosaur bones and eggs, learn about the California Indians and pat a live chicken and pig. They can also peek into a salt water aquarium, talk to crows and mynah birds, handle various minerals and ores and explore electricity. The members of the Golden Gate Model-Railroad Club, which is located downstairs in this building, allow the public to watch their play with the model trains on the huge room-sized track.

Josephine Randall Junior Museum

Golden Gate Park

From Stanyan St. west to the ocean; use Eighth Ave. entrance (at Fulton St.) to main part of park. Tel. 558-3706, McLaren Lodge, Lost & Found, check S.F. Recreation Listings for individual phone numbers.

● There are over 1,000 acres of lakes and greenery in San Francisco's Golden Gate Park and at least 100 things to see and do. You can go boating or feed the ducks in the lakes and ponds, cheer toy sailboat races, picnic, ride horses, play tennis, golf or handball, go lawn bowling, watch the grazing buffalo and elk, bicycle, watch soccer and polo matches, pitch horseshoes, shoot arrows, play cards or chess, practice fly casting or *petanque* (French lawn bowling) or make water rings in the fountains. Wander with older children through *Shakespeare's Garden* to identify the plants he wrote of — from wormwood and yew to bilberry and eglantine. Climb the moon bridge in the *Japanese Tea Garden* (open 8 A.M.-dusk), then sit down to tea and cookies in the *Japanese Tea House* (30¢). Wonder at the tulips blooming in *Queen Wilhelmina's Gardens* (near the ocean) in late April. Say thank you to John McLaren for the park when the rhododendrons bloom in his dell. Browse through the candycake and spun sugar Victorian *Conservatory* (open 8 A.M.-4:30 P.M.; tel. 558-3973; free) at any time of the year to see displays of potted flowers. Ring the Mexican Bell in the *Strybing Arboretum's Garden of Fragrance*, where you can also test your powers of smell, touch and taste (open weekdays, 8 A.M.-4:30 P.M.; weekends, 10 A.M.-5 P.M.). Gaze at the *Portals of the Past*, the marble columns that once were all that was left of a Nob Hill mansion after the earthquake, and now stand over a duck-filled lake. There is something here in this wonderful park for every imagination. Have a good time!

M.H.deYoung Memorial Museum

Golden Gate Park, north side of Music Concourse, Tel. 558-2887. Daily, 10 A.M.-5 P.M. Persons 18-65, 75¢; 12-18, 25¢. Free 1st day of each month.

• The deYoung's romantic Pool of Enchantment, with water lilies and a sculpted boy playing his pipes to two mountain lions, beckons visitors to a land of enchantment. There are paintings, sculpture, tapestries and graphics by American, Californian and European artists. The Rembrandts are shown without fanfare, and there is a lovely Mary Cassatt in the modern section. Children especially like the "real rooms" — the muraled boudoir from Italy and the Elizabethan paneled bedroom. Our favorite painting is the huge "Rainy Day in the Tropics" by Frederick Church, in which a rainbow arches over a tropical rain forest. The new gallery of the arts of Africa, Oceania and the Americas features a 14' totem pole from Alaska.

California Academy of Sciences

The Asian Art Museum next-door is a fascinating and beautifully arranged collection of oriental jade, scrolls, sculpture and jewelry.

California Academy of Sciences

Golden Gate Park, south side of Music Concourse. Tel. 221-5100. Daily, 10 A.M.-9 P.M., summer; 10 A.M.-5 P.M., winter. Adults, 50¢; ages 12-18, 25¢; under 12, free. Planetarium shows: daily, 12:30, 2, 3:30 and and 8 P.M., summer; daily, 2 P.M. Wed.-Sun., 8 P.M., winter. Adults, $1.50; under 16, 50¢.

● Wander through the Hall of North American Mammals, the Hall of Minerals with its histories of photography, earthquakes and geology, and the Hall of North American Birds with its model of the Farallon Island bird rookery, or you might want to head for the Hall of Fossils with dinosaur bones, Brontops skulls and a whale skeleton. A photo demonstration of museum-staff field work and the steps taken in preparing animals for exhibit in natural settings tells you how museum people work.

A whale fountain courtyard, inhabited by crocodiles and alligators is the central meeting point. Behind it, in the *Steinhart Aquarium*, over 14,500 fish, reptiles and dolphins live in 243 colorful tanks. The glass cases are low enough for children to see in easily — and when they aren't, there are boxes to climb up on. Seahorses, deadly stonefish, dolphins that sound like Flipper, seals, Amazon manatees eating lettuce, piranhas, and shellfish of all colors, shapes and sizes live here. An artificial tidepool, with water flowing in and out like waves, is remarkable. The fish are fed at 1:30 P.M.; dolphins get a meal every two hours, starting at 10:30 A.M.

The Hall of Man in Nature, two African Halls, a Hall of Botany and a Hall of Space Science are located in the third wing of the Academy, along with an African waterhole and Audubon birds. *Morrison Planetarium* shows moon photos, time machines and all the stars and galaxies.

The Exploratorium

Palace of Fine Arts, Lyon St. Tel. 563-7337. Wed.-Sun., 1-5 P.M.; Wed., eve., 7-9:30 P.M. Free.

● The technology of modern science is on display here to challenge and confound youngsters (and most adults as well). It is not a place to just stand and watch. Visitors are expected to touch and hear, see and explore, improvise and play with whatever attracts them. Children can test laser beams and holograms, figure out the principles of stereophonic sound, gaze at an eternally moving pendulum, or work with radio and television sets, kaleidoscopes and strobe lights. We liked the whole exhibit very much but were especially intrigued with the tactile gallery labyrinth (reservations necessary), and the platform that spins faster as you raise one leg.

You and your youngsters will also enjoy watching the ducks and swans in the lagoon. The Palace, recently restored, was designed by Bernard Maybeck for the 1915 Exposition; this is one of San Francisco's most romantic and beautiful spots.

Presidio Army Museum

Funston & Lincoln Blvds., Presidio. Tel. 561-4115 Tues.-Sun., 10 A.M.-4 P.M. Free.

● Two hundred years of military history of the West are represented under the flags of Spain, Mexico and the United States (flags that flew over San Francisco). The uniform collection dates back to 1846.

Fort Point

Foot of Marine Drive (under S.F. end of the Golden Gate Bridge), The Presidio. Tel. 556-1693. Daily, 10 A.M.-5 P.M. Hourly guided tours on weekends. Free.

● Nestled below the underpinnings of the Golden Gate Bridge, Fort Point, built during the Civil War, is the only brick seacoast fortress in the west — the guardian of San Francisco Bay. With the icy Pacific slamming into the retaining wall and the wind whistling around the point, this is one of the coldest spots in San Francisco and you can understand why this place was used as a detention barracks and a "hardship tour" by the army up until World War II. The children will enjoy their close-up view of the small cannons scattered under the courtyard

shelters and the dismal jail, which hasn't changed much in more than a century, nor have the spiral granite steps that lead up to the second floor. The museum rooms display swords, guns, compasses, shells, cannon balls, chains and handcuffs. You can also find an eyewitness account of the assassination of President Lincoln, relics of the San Francisco earthquake, 19th- century medical supplies and a Confederate soldier's uniform and flag.

Palace of the Legion of Honor

Lincoln Park, off 34th Ave. and Clement St. Tel. 558-2881. Daily, 10 A.M.-5 P.M. Persons 18-65, 75¢; ages 12-18, 25¢. Free 1st day of each month.

● This impressive marble building features Rodin's "The Thinker" in the courtyard and houses an inviting collection of works by Degas, Fragonard, Manet, Monet, Renoir, and several 20th-century printmakers. Sunday afternoon organ concerts make this a special place to visit. The best thing here for children is the location. Land's End is on the grounds of the museum and you can get a thrilling view from here of the Golden Gate Bridge from the ocean side.

The Book Place

50 Clement. Tel. 752-4800. Mon.-Sat. 10 A.M.-6 P.M.; Sun. 1-6 P.M.

● A brilliant Peter Max-like mural announces this multi-leveled color-

Fort Point

ful book store devoted to children — the only one in Northern California devoted to kids books from pre-school to high school levels. The people who run the place really like children and designed the place just for them. There are funhouse mirrors, a fireplace to cuddle up in front of, loft space that's too short for adults, and displays of antique toys. The children are welcome to browse at will and read as long as they like. Many youngsters introduce their parents to the place after visiting with a school group. If you want to encourage your kids to read, The Book Place is the place to go.

Polly Ann's Exotic Flavors

3142 Noriega St., Tel. 664-2472. Daily, noon-10 P.M.; Fri. and Sat., to 11 P.M.

● This small neighborhood ice cream shop rates special mention because of the quality and rare flavors of ice cream available — American Beauty Rose, Chinese Ginger, Fruit Cake, Happy (pop) Corn, Pistachio-Melon Salad, Sunflower Seed (salty), tart lemonade, cinnamonny Chocolate Sombrero, Peanut Butter and Marshmallow. More flavors like pizza, black olive and hot chili are in the works. The top price in the store is $1.40 for the Psychedelic Sundae — eight flavors of ice cream and toppings, served in a huge glass that you can keep. The best feature of all: every dog and every child under five gets a special cone of his own — free.

Cliff House

1066 Point Lobos Ave. Tel. 751-7219. Daily, 9 A.M.-6 P.M.

● The Cliff House is a San Francisco landmark that has burned down too many times and is now more than a little seedy around the edges. But it's still the best place in town to see the Seal Rocks, covered with barking seals. Downstairs, handcarved models of the 21 California missions are shown for 10¢, (on weekends) and the musee Mecanique — a large room full of old-time coin-operated movies, games, music machines, Swiss Music boxes and mechanical wonders — will while away many hours and dimes. P.T. Barnum's collection of mechanical carnivals is the best machine to play.

San Francisco Zoo

Sloat Blvd. and the Great Highway. Tel. 661-4844. Daily, 10 A.M.-6 P.M., summer; 10 A.M.-5 P.M., winter. Adults, 50¢; under 15, 15¢; free days, 1st, 3rd, & 4th Tues. and 2nd Sat. of month. Storyland & Petting Zoo: Adults, 35¢; children; 25¢. Lifetime Zoo Key: 50¢ (operates tapes giving history, biology and interesting anecdotes about animals).

● Animals from all over the world live here in naturalistic settings. There are cassowary birds and wallaroos, snow leopards, okapis, spectacled bears, flamingos, seals, emus, koalas, Moulon and Barbary sheep, strutting peacocks and proud reindeer. All are clearly named and described, and birds are identified by picture as well. The main aviary building is a tropical rain forest (open 11 A.M.-3 P.M. daily) in which you can walk amid the more than 85 species of birds from pigeons to curassows. Lions are fed at 2, leopards at 2:45 daily. The elephants bathe at 1 P.M. on Sundays. For youngsters who grow impatient with the bird watching, there are spaceship rides and a cable car and locomotive to climb

through. In Storyland, kids can climb up the Old Woman's Shoe and slide out the top window, snack at the Mad Hatter's Munch Bar and play in a land of nursery rhymes with real animals — Mary's Little Lamb, the Three Little Pigs and Peter Rabbit — there to be petted. The Zoo is right near the ocean, so it's wise to always have sweaters on hand.

Public Relations Tours

Foremost Foods Co.

366 Guerrero St. Tel. 431-6000. Free tours (by appt.).

● See how ice cream and other dairy products are made or handled.

Raggedy Robin & the Magical Miracle Circus Museum

Tel. 751-0217. Visits by appt.

● Circus artifacts — costumes, posters, and masks — from 19th and 20th century circuses are now at home with Raggedy Robin. A formal address will be arranged by next summer.

K-101 FM Radio

700 Montgomery St. Tel. 456-5101. Free tours (by appt.).

● See the new pyramid-shaped Transamerica skyscraper while visiting this radio studio with the first four-channel stereo facility in California.

KNBR

Fox Plaza Tel. 626-6700. Free tours (by appt.) 9-5 weekdays.

● In half an hour, visitors can see studios, control rooms, news, sales and FM automation equipment during their tour.

KSFO Radio

950 California St. Tel. 982-5500. Free tours (by appt.) mid-morning or mid-afternoon.

● See news production, the music library, traffic continuity and a disk jockey in action.

KYA

1 Nob Hill Circle, Pine and Mason Sts. Tel. 397-2500. Free tours (by appt.)

● Tours take you through broadcast studio, control room, production room, news room and FM facilities.

Golden Gate Ferry to Sausalito

36

2

MARIN COUNTY

Marin County is a land of mountains and seashore, north of the Golden Gate Bridge. Most of the "places" to go with children in Marin are natural wonders. You can drive to the top of Mt. Tamalpais and walk the trails overlooking miles of ocean, land and city. You can explore the silent redwood groves of Muir Woods, then travel on to Stinson or one of the quieter beaches for a seaside picnic, rock-hunting and driftwood-collecting, or even a quick dip in the cold sea. You can also spend profitable hours fishing in the Marin lakes, or hiking the beautiful Point Reyes National Seashore area. And when you feel the need for civilization you can head for Tiburon or Sausalito, where the children will be as enchanted as you by the appearance and attractions of these bayside villages.

Sausalito

● Noted for years as an artists' colony, the village of Sausalito today is a mecca for tourists and young people. There are clothing and gift shops, ice cream parlors and art galleries, coffee houses and restaurants for every age, taste, and budget. Visitors can climb up the stairs from the main street to the *Alta Mira* (126 Harrison Ave., 332-1350, 8 A.M.-9 P.M.) for an elegant brunch (Eggs Benedict and salads, $3.50, pancakes with blueberry sauce, $2.15) or dinner and a breathtaking view of San Francisco. Rock fans (like my 11- and 12-year-old nephews) might prefer the pseudo-health-hip *Trident* (558 Bridgeway, 332-1334, 11 A.M.-2 A.M.). Hamburgers, soups, salads, and quiche are usually under $4. Fast-foods places line Bridgeway, for stand-up dining. Be sure to take your children to *Shelby Gallery* (673 Bridgeway, 332-4991) to see the vast collection of Navaho jewelry and turquoise. The best way to get to Sausalito, in terms of enjoyment and Sausalito's crowded parking space, is to take the *Golden Gate Ferry*.

Bay & Delta Scale Model

2100 Bridgeway, Sausalito, Tel. 332-3870. Mon.-Fri., 1st & 3rd Sats., 9 A.M.-4 P.M. Groups by appt. Free.

● The U.S. Army Corps of Engineers has put together a hydraulic scale model of San Francisco Bay and the Sacramento-San Joaquin Delta. The model shows the action of the tides, the flow and currents of the water, and the mixing of sea water and fresh water. Group tours take 1½ hours, but individuals can use the self-guided recorded tour system to see the exhibit at their own speed. It's a good idea to call first — the model is not always "in action."

Tiburon

● Tiburon, a quiet, one-street bayside village, is a nice place to spend a sunny afternoon. While the adults sit peacefully enjoying a drink and the view from one of the many restaurants along Main Street, the kids can spend hours at the *Musee Mecanique* (boardwalk, 10 A.M.-6 P.M. Dozens of old music boxes, movies, and games entertain as long as the nickels and dimes hold out. We were especially taken with the mechanical music box depicting the seven lands of the after-world from Chinese myth. The nautical shops, Swedish bakery, book store, and spice store are all fun to browse through. Hardy walkers can head up the hill to *The Landmark Society Museum* in St. Hilary's Church (tel. 435-1853; Sun. and Wed., 1-4 P.M., Apr.-Oct., free & by appt.). A changing art exhibit, specimens of local plants, a board of sailors' knots and a small collection of Marin County gems and minerals are on view. Many rare plants grow in the churchyard, including two found nowhere else in the world — the Black Jewel and the Tiburon Paintbrush.

Angel Island State Park

In San Francisco Bay. Tel. 435-1915 A.M.-dusk. 25¢ (part of ferry fare). For ferry information from San Francisco, see page 26.

● Secluded picnic groves, beaches, forest trails and historic military buildings, make Angel Island a wonderful place to spend the day. The historic buildings are now being reconstructed. There are plenty of deer and sea birds to keep youngsters busy. On weekends, the island tour bus leaves the barbecue area at 11:30 A.M., 2, and 3 P.M. for hour-long jaunts around the island ($1.50 adults, 75¢ children). The Angel Island State Park Ferry leaves the Main Street dock in Tiburon hourly from 10 A.M. on weekends (tel. 435-2131; round trip: adults: $1.75; ages 5-11, $1). During the week, the only way to get to Angel Island (unless you have your own boat) is to join a charter group on the Angel Island State Park Ferry.

Muir Woods National Monument

Off Hwy. 1, on Muir Woods Road. Tel. 388-2595. Daily, 8 A.M. to sunset. Adults, 50¢; under 16 & over 62; free.

● This lovely forest of giant Coast redwoods, some over 200 feet, is a wonderful place for an early morning walk. Among these magnificent trees, you'll encounter many other species of plant life — azalea, red alder and California laurels — as well as an occasional black-tailed deer hiding in the dark ferns, squirrels scampering across the trail and, from spring to autumn, young salmon and trout swimming through Redwood Creek. Although the main inner trail of the forest is concrete-covered for protection, the outer trails are natural earth for easy walking. A self-guiding nature trail along Redwood Creek helps visitors understand the forest and blind visitors should be sure to walk the Braille Trail. A lunch counter, gift shop and ranger's station are located near the entrance of the park.

Louise A. Boyd Museum of Science

76 Albert Park Lane, San Rafael. Tel. 454-6961. Tues.-Sat., 10 A.M.-5 P.M. Donations. Sea food, 25¢; raccoon food, 10¢.

● This museum is a wildlife rehabilitation and nature education center. The wildlife program helps injured and orphaned wildlife so they can be released back into their natural habitats. Those on exhibit, such as the black bear, badger, red fox, ravens, owls and hawks are not releasable. Inside, youngsters will enjoy the "touch me room," the exhibit on the Indians found on the Marin County coast by Sir Francis Drake and the displays on wasps and ecology. There are always new exhibits. Dioramas of Marin County's forest, salt marsh, chaparral, seashore and grasslands exhibit the animals of the area. A model of a Miwok village shows men making weapons and women grinding acorns. The gift and book shop has a remarkably good collection of shells that are fun to look at.

Marin County Historical Society Museum

1125 B St., Boyd Park, San Rafael. Tel. 545-8538. Wed.-Sun., 1-4 P.M. Free.

• The thing the kids liked best was the huge tallow kettle at the entrance gate. Once used for taking tallow from Elk at the Rancho Olompali in the time of the vaqueros, the kettle was also used as a stewpot for the military during the Bear Flag War. The youngsters thought it made a great hiding place. An 1880's wedding shawl, an early San Quentin oil lamp, Lillie Coit's high button shoes, maps of the original Mexican land grants and mementos of the Miwoks, Mexicans and pioneers who settled Marin are on display inside the museum.

Just down the block is the back entrance to the Mission San Rafael Archangel (1104 5th Ave., tel. 456-3016). We had 15 minutes to spend while waiting to get into the museum, and visiting the mission takes just about that long. At one end of the mission gift shop there is a display of mission furniture, elegant Spanish tapestries and candelabra. Photos of the mission in all stages of reconstruction are on the walls and Indian arrowheads and beads, priests' garments and municipal records from 1817 on are displayed in the window cabinets outside the building. The unassuming chapel flies the 6 flags under which the mission has served: Spain, Mexico, the California Republic, United States of 1850, the Vatican and the United States.

Audubon Canyon Ranch

Hwy. 1, 2½ miles north of Stinson Beach. Tel. 383-1644. Sat., Sun. and holidays, 10 A.M.-4 P.M., Mar.-July: Free.

• This 1,000-acre wildlife sanctuary bordering on the Bolinas Lagoon is a peaceful, beautiful spot to view birds "at home." From a hilltop, watch the nesting activities of the Great Blue Heron and Great Egret in the treetops below you. The ranch's pond, stream and canyon are a living demonstration of the region's ecology: the delicate balance between plant and animal life and their environment. A display hall houses exhibits of local fauna and flora, the San Andreas fault and photos of the birds and their home. An area on the grounds has been set aside for picnics.

Point Reyes National Seashore

Hwy. 1, Olema. Tel. 663-1092. Daily, 8 A.M.-sundown. Free.

• Sir Francis Drake is said to have landed here in 1579. The sharp cliffs, swimmable and unswimmable surf, streams, tidepools, lowlands, and forest meadows make you wonder why he went back to England. You can watch the bird rookeries in the trees and sea lion rocks just off shore. You can walk along four well-marked nature trails, hike through miles of untouched land, backpack, camp (by reservation in special areas only), and picnic. The information center at Olema has a small natural history exhibit and aquarium and the Parks Department raises Morgan horses right next door. Prices vary for camping, riding and parking, but all are very reasonable. We like Drake's Beach best and before we set out we call the ranger's office there (699-1250) to make sure it's sunny.

Tomales Bay State Park (Inverness, Tel. (415) 699-1140 daily, 8 A.M.-8 P.M. summer; 8 A.M.-6 P.M., (parking, 75¢) is part of the Point Reyes National Seashore. Craggy Bishop pines, sandy beaches, and over 300 different species of plants, animals and birds attract nature lovers. Tidepooling is a favorite pastime here. Tidepools are the rocky pockets which retain sea-water when the tide goes out. Many strange animals and plants live among their rocks — seaweeds, anemones, barnacles, worms, jellyfish, shellfish, sand dollars, sea urchins, and tiny fish and algae. The best way to look at a tidepool is to lie very quietly until the tidepool's occupants think you're part of the landscape and continue to move through their daily paces. Tidepool animals may not be collected by youngsters, but they will provide many engrossing hours.

Marin French Cheese Co.

7500 Red Hill Rd. Petaluma (9 miles west of Novato, at Novato Blvd.). Tel. 762-6001. Sales room, with tasting, open daily, 10 A.M.-5 P.M. Tours 10 A.M.-4 P.M. Free.

● The makers of Rouge et Noir cheeses are situated next to a pond in the rolling, cow-speckled hills between Novato and the coast. It is a perfect destination for an afternoon outing and a picnic. The Marin French Cheese Company has been in the same pioneer family for over 100 years. The 15-minute tour through the factory begins with the 4,000-gallon tank of milk and takes you right through the different stages of cheese making — heating the milk, adding the three "cheese" ingredients (culture, enzymes and starter), and aging. You pass shiny steel tubes and tanks, a strange Rube Goldberg-type machine that makes the cheese boxes, and several different aging rooms, each with its own special smells. You may sample the Rouge et Noir cheeses — Breakfast Camembert, Brie and Schloss — in the salesroom, where you may also purchase "irregular cuts" of the cheeses at cut-rate prices. Sausages, breads, soda and ice cream are available for impromptu picnics.

Novato Prehistory Museum

2200 Novato Blvd., Miwok Park, Novato. Tel 897-4064. Sat. 10 A.M.-4 P.M.; Sun. noon-4 P.M. & by appt. Free.

● Native American artifacts are used to illustrate the prehistoric period of the Marin County area. The culture of the Coast Miwoks is represented by decorated baskets, cooking implements, arrowheads and ceremonial charm stones shaped like fish. Picnic facilities available.

3

NAPA, SONOMA, AND LAKE COUNTIES

Napa, Sonoma and Lake counties are best known for the vineyards that grow on the rolling hills and in the Valley of the Moon — and for the wineries. Wineries can be fun for children to visit, not only because the wine-making process is fascinating, but because the wine industry is part of California's history and culture. In most wineries, your tour will follow the direction the grape takes, from delivery from the vineyards, to the crushing, to the aging vat, to the bottles in the tasting rooms. The listed wineries offer the most interesting plants and tours, all of which are free (including the "tasting" for the old folks).

Yountville-Vintage 1870

Hwy. 29, Yountville. Tel. 944-2788. Daily, 10 A.M.-6 P.M.

● This lovely old former winery is part of an original land grant made to Salvador Vallejo in 1838 and was bought in 1870 for $250 in U.S. gold coin. The brick exterior of the building hasn't changed much in the past century, but the interior is now a charming complex of shops, theater, galleries, restaurants, candle and candy makers, potters, a glass blower and a leather craftsman, who work in open stores. The Chutney Kitchen offers tastes of their unique relishes.

Robert Mondavi Winery

Hwy. 29, Oakville. Tel. 963-7156. Daily tours, 10 A.M.-4 P.M. Free.

• Designed and landscaped by Cliff May, the same architect who designed the Sunset Magazine buildings, the newly built Mondavi winery is a beautiful place to visit. Your tour takes you from the holding tanks, where grapes are dumped from the fields, past conveyor belts, cleaners and crushers. Huge wooden tanks stand in cool cellars. Smaller barrels of French oak and redwood store the red and white wines until they're ready for bottling. Jazz and chamber music concerts and special events are frequently held on summer Sundays on the center lawn.

Napa Valley Olive Oil Manufactory

Charter Oak Rd. at end of McCorkle Ave., St. Helena. Tel. 963-4173. Daily, 8 A.M.-6:30 P.M.

• A visit to the Napa Valley wineries is not complete without a stop at this old-fashioned olive oil factory and sausage and cheese store. Hidden at the end of a block on the southern entrance to town, the factory looks more like a deserted barn than the bustling business that you find inside. The front room is filled with long counters holding vast amounts of all kinds, shapes and colors of cheese. Several varieties of sausages age on hooks in the back room or rest in barrels next to the stacks of bottled olive oil and tinned Italian delicacies. The children will enjoy the quaintness and bustle and wonderful smells of the store, while you supplement the picnic lunch with cheeses and salami at bargain prices. Occasionally, local bakers offer tastes of their desserts.

The Silverado Museum

1347 Railroad Ave., St. Helena. Tel. 963-3757. Daily ex. Mon. and holidays, noon-4 P.M. Free.

• Robert Louis Stevenson has been associated with the Napa Valley ever since he spent a penniless honeymoon in an abandoned bunkhouse of the Silverado Mine on nearby Mount St. Helena. Today, anyone who grew up on *A Child's Garden of Verses* or *Treasure Island, Kidnapped* or *Dr. Jekyll and Mr. Hyde* will appreciate this tribute to the man who wrote them. Portraits of Stevenson in photograph, painting and sculpture abound, including one by his mother showing Robert as a fair young boy with long flowing curls. Original manuscripts and illustrations, the author's toy lead soldiers, a child's tea set, a hammock and other things from his plantation in Samoa are among the Stevensonia on display. Friendly and knowledgeable docents are on hand to answer questions.

Tour the wineries

Christian Brothers Winery

Hwy. 29, St. Helena. Tel. 963-2719. Daily tours, 10:30 A.M.-4 P.M. Free.

● This imposing castle, the largest stone winery in the world, is the center for the good Brothers' wine aging and champagne cellar. If you want to see how the monks make wines to support schools and colleges throughout America, this is where to go. A large part of Brother Timothy's cork screw collection is on view.

Sterling Vinyards

1111 Dunaweal Lane, Calistoga. Tel. 942-5151. Daily, 10:30 A.M.-5 P.M.

● Tours via aerial tramway, past overhead galleries and unusual visitor exhibits.

Freemark Abbey

Hwy. 29, 3020 St. Helena Hwy. North, Tel. 963-7211. Mon.-Fri., 10 A.M.-5 P.M.; weekends, to 6 P.M. Free.

● The old Freemark Abbey Winery building now houses the Hurd Beeswax Candle Factory and gift shop and a small winery. Weekday visitors may see the candlemakers working until 4:30 P.M. On the far wall of the inside showroom, a wooden shutter opens to reveal the back of a beehive full of bees filling their honeycomb. Every imaginable color, kind and shape of candle is featured on tables and shelves in two large rooms. Gourmet books and cookery supplies, cheese, ice cream and tasty snacks and delicacies are available in the gourmet shop. You can pick up some of the fixings for a picnic here. The winery offers tastings and a short tour.

The Old Bale Mill

Hwy. 29, St. Helena. Daily, 9 A.M.-4:30 P.M. in winter; 10 A.M.-6 P.M. in summer. Free.

● Dr. E.T. Bale built this grist mill in 1846, and flour was last ground here in 1879 with the help of pioneers. The buildings and waterwheels were reconstructed with some of the original equipment and timbers still intact. Youngsters can climb through the old wooden building and follow the milling process with typed explanations and envision how early settlers made flour.

Napa County Historical Society

Napa County Fairgrounds, 1435 Oak St., Calistoga. Tel. 963-4023. Sat. and Sun., noon to 3 P.M. & by appt. Free.

● If you are in the area on a weekend, stop at the Napa County Fairgrounds and spend a few minutes in the Historical Society's tribute to the last century. Although the collection is small and mostly unlabeled, the 19th-century household goods, some displayed in model rooms, give a vivid picture of life in the valley in the 1800s. Dolls with their own dishes and furniture, a sleigh-shaped bed and a melodious collection of 500 bells caught the attention of our youngsters. Scrapbooks and Robert Louis Stevenson remembrances, farming tools from Scotland and the beads, arrowheads and papoose baskets of local Indians further illuminate the period.

Old Faithful Geyser of California

Tubbs Lane, Calistoga. Open daily, 8 A.M. to sundown, weather permitting. Adults $1; ages 6-14, 50¢.

● One of the three "faithful" geysers in the world, this one erupts 350-degree water about every 40 minutes to a height ranging from 50 to 200 feet. The geyser rumbles, belches forth a small fountain, rum-

Old Faithful Geyser

bles for about 4 minutes more and then gushes forth with a rainbow of foaming steam and water. The geyser's height and the number of rainbows it makes depends on the intensity of the wind. A tape gives historical and geological aspects and tells how geysers, and especially faithful geysers, are formed. Picnic tables are in a good position for the view. The owners use another geyser on their property to heat their house, and there is a wishing well nearby with 130-degree water.

The Petrified Forest

Petrified Forest Rd., west of Calistoga. Tel. 942-6667. Daily 9 A.M.-5 P.M. $1.50. Under 10, free.

● This forest of petrified giant redwoods, formed by the volcanic eruptions of Mt. St. Helena 6 million years ago, was discovered in 1870. Visitors walk along a lovely forest trail to the various sites of the partly dug-up stone giants. Among the most spectacular are the 300-foot-long "Monarch" tunnel tree and "the Giant" that was already 3,000 years old when it was buried millions of years ago. Robert Louis Stevenson mentioned the forest in *The Silverado Squatters* and the owners are still very proud of this. On the way out, you'll walk through a specimen shop of fossils and petrified worms, snails, clams, nuts and wood.

Petaluma Adobe

3325 Adobe Rd., Petaluma (east of Hwy. 101). Tel. 762-4871. Daily, 10

A.M.-5 P.M. *Adult ticket, 25¢, usable at all state parks that day.*

● General Mariano G. Vallejo's ranch house, Casa Grande, was built in 1836 as the centerpiece of a Mexican land grant of 66,000 acres. Here we learned that adobe means, in Spanish, "to mix" and that the thick, naturally insulating bricks were made from clay mixed in water with straw and then dried in the sun. Visitors walk through the adobe on a self-guided tour. The kitchen, workshop, candle room, weaving room, servants' quarters and The Vallejos' living quarters upstairs are graciously furnished with some of the original pieces. Outside, there are huge iron cauldrons and the racks on which hides — a currency of the period — were stretched out to dry. At one time, General Vallejo had 1,000 workers on the ranch, and it's not hard, standing before the Casa Grande today, to imagine the bustle of yesteryear.

Sonoma State Historic Park

Spain St. and First St. East, Tel. 938-4779. Daily 10 A.M.-5 P.M. Adult ticket, 25¢, usable at all state parks that day.

● *Lachryma Montis*, at 3rd St. above West Spain St., was General Vallejo's "city house." The house is furnished precisely as it was when he lived there with his family, right down to the photo of Abraham Lincoln on the wall. One daughter's painting is on the wall, along with family photos and Catholic mementos. Behind the house is the kitchen building and the Chinese cook's quarters. Across the garden is the "Chalet," once the storehouse and now a Vallejo museum containing his books, pictures, saddles, coach and cattle brand, various mementos of the family and biographies of ten of his sixteen children.

On the plaza at Spain St. and 1st St. East is the two-story *Sonoma Barracks*, erected in 1840 to garrison the soldiers, first of Mexico and then of the United States after the Bear Flag Revolt. Visitors may walk upstairs to see the barracks, but most of the building is still being reconstructed.

Blue Wing Inn, across the street, was once a hotel visited by John Fremont, Kit Carson, Generals Grant, Sherman and P. Smith, and the bandit Joaquin Murietta. Now it's a complex of antique and craft shops.

The Mission San Francisco Solano at East Spain St. and 1st St. East was the last and most northerly of the 21 Franciscan missions in California and the only one established under Mexican rule. The adobe padres' quarters is the oldest structure in Sonoma. Visitors can walk through the buildings to see water colors of the other missions, several simply furnished rooms of the padres, maps of the Indian tribes, spurs and leggings of the vaqueros and other interesting artifacts from the mission life. The primitively painted chapel is also of interest. Don't forget to walk across the plaza to see the old stone *Sonoma City Hall*.

Lachryma Montis – General Vallejo's home

Sonoma County Farm Trails

P.O. Box 6043, Santa Rosa, CA 95406. Free map.

• Drive from a Mushroom Farm & the Eggery in Petaluma to the Apple Tree in Sebastopol or tour neighboring farms in an authentic horse-drawn carriage, from surry to stagecoach, via 101 Carriage Charter, 3325 Hwy. 116 N., Sebastapol 95472 (823-7083). In winter, you may want to cut your own Christmas trees. For Christmas Tree Farm Listings write to California Christmas Tree Growers, 2855 Telegraph Ave., Berkeley, CA 94705.

Buena Vista Winery

Old Winery Rd., Sonoma. Tel. 938-8504. Open daily. 9 A.M.-5 P.M., for self-guided tour. Free.

• Buena Vista was the first winery with stone wine cellars in California. Founded in 1857 by a Hungarian, Count Agoston Haraszthy, who made the first commercial importation of European grape varieties, the Buena Vista Winery is now a California historical landmark.

Sebastiani Vineyards

389 East 4th St., Sonoma. Tel. 938-5532. Daily tours, 10 A.M.-5 P.M. Free.

• The Sebastiani winery is another state historical landmark, commemorated as one of the oldest vineyards in Northern California.

Tours take you past redwood tanks and carved oak casks. This third generation winery, now storing 2 million gallons of wine, began with a 500 gallon tank and some primitive equipment. It is known for its red Barbera table wine. The children will be most interested in the huge vats and the old carved oak casks.

Traintown

Broadway, Sonoma. Tel. 938-3912. 10:30 A.M.-5:30 P.M. Daily from Mid-June to Labor Day, weekends in winter. Adults, $2; children, $1.

• Traintown is a railroad park and the home of the Sonoma Steam RR, a quarter-size reproduction of a mountain division steam railroad of the 1890s. A 15-minute trip takes you over high trestles and into Traintown, stopping to take on water in Lakeville, a miniature ¼-scale mining town. While you listen to a recorded history of the "town," you can wander around the buildings, and feel like Gulliver. This 10-acre railroad park is a recollection of the golden age of Western railroading.

Jack London State Historic Park

Glen Ellen, Tel. 938-5216. Daily, 10 A.M.-5 P.M. Adult ticket, 25¢.

• Charmian London built the House of Happy Walls as a memorial to her husband. Furnished with the furniture and art gathered for Wolf House, which burned before the Londons could move into it, this museum thoroughly covers the life of the adventurous young man. Once a sailor, prospector and roustabout, London struggled to be accepted as a writer. The collection even includes some of London's rejection slips. Lining the walls are photos of the Snark, in which Jack and Charmian sailed the South Pacific, and treasures collected on their voyage. There are wood carvings and war spears, tapa cloth from the Marquesas Islands, dancing sticks from the Solomons and many Polynesian artifacts. Books sold by the ranger are stamped with London's signature (the stamp he used to save time).

A 1¼-mile trail leads from the House of Happy Walls to the fieldstone ruins of Wolf House. Along the trail you'll see a display of farm implements used by London and his friends, as well as his bouldermarked grave.

The World of Jack London
Jack London Village

14300 Arnold Drive, Glen Ellen. Tel. 996-2888. Tues.-Sun., 10 A.M.-6 P.M.

• Located in a marvelous book shop specializing in books by Jack London and his friends, this unique museum is a collection of posters made for movies of London's books, plaques, pictures, dishes, memorial cups, scrapbooks, and remembrances. The collection has been visited by many famous people, and even the guest book makes amusing reading. The shopping complex itself is a restored flour mill and winery owned at one time by Jack London. Juanita's Galley is now open in the Village.

Italian Swiss Colony Winery

Hwy. 101, Asti. Tel. 894-2541. Tours daily, 8:30 A.M.-5:30 P.M., summer; 9:30 A.M.-4 P.M., winter. Free.

• A tour through Italian Swiss Colony is especially interesting to people who think all wineries are small, old-fashioned operations. It might be a disappointment to those who still believe in "That Little Old Wine Maker." He's been replaced by a white-coated scientist. At Italian Swiss Colony you'll see stainless steel tanks, shiny pipes and chemistry laboratories that suggest that winemaking is a science rather than an art. Junior scientists will enjoy this visit, and not just for the free postcards and cookies. Picnic grounds are available for guests.

Sonoma County Historical Museum & Codding Natural History Museum

557 Summerfield Rd., Santa Rosa. Tel. 539-0556. Tues., Thurs., Sat. and Sun., 1-5 P.M. Free.

• A stuffed Bengal tiger greets you at the entrance to this interesting dual museum. One part of the building features the history of Sonoma County; the other shows the wildlife of the world. Old photos of the county and San Francisco before and after 1906, a 1902 Sears Roebuck catalog, the Delft plate sent by the Dutch in 1947 as thanks to Santa Rosa's children for 3,000 pounds of clothing in a war-relief drive, the first Santa Rosa entry (1966) to the Soap Box Derby — these are among the many items in the cluttered historical collection. In the wildlife museum, the natural dioramas of veldt, waterhole and seashore are nicely put together, and the children were quite taken with the Big Horn mountain goats, caribou and polar bears mounted on the walls.

Ripley's Believe It or Not Memorial Museum

Juilliard Park, Santa Rosa Ave., Santa Rosa. Tel. 545-1414. Daily, 11 A.M.-5 P.M.; May-Sept; 11 A.M.-4 P.M.; Oct.-April. Adults, 25¢; under 12, 10¢.

● Nestled in tall redwoods, this little church, built from *one* tree, houses the personal articles and original drawings and papers of the Santa Rosa native who coined the phrase "Believe It or Not." The wax figure of Ripley at his desk looks out at cases of personal memorabilia — comic and pocket books of his features, photos of him with Will Rogers and Shirley Temple, newspaper clippings — as well as samplings of the oddities and curiosities he collected. If he's not too busy, the guard will play one of Ripley's radio programs from the 1930s.

The *Luther Burbank Memorial Garden* is across the street for those school children who may have read about this noted botanist. A kiosk in the center of the garden displays some of his tools and tells the story of his life.

Charlene's Yesterdays' Museum

Bodega Hwy., Bodega. Tel. 876-3282. Wed.-Sun. 11 A.M.-5 P.M.; Adults 50¢, children 25¢.

● Hundreds of antique dolls, toys, curios, and memories are crammed into the spacious barn. Santa's toy shop looks ready for production, and Granma's kitchen is just one display area, as is the old schoolroom. There are French, German and Japanese dolls, Shirley Temple dolls and books, the Good Ship Lollipop, Jeanette MacDonald, musical and mechanical dolls and old-time playthings along with Lily Langtry and old movie mementos and stuffed animals. Picnic in a shady nook and listen to the tapping drums and crashing cymbals of an authentic player piano.

Union Hotel Restaurant

Occidental, Tel. 874-3662. Daily, noon-9 P.M.

● Dining at the Union Hotel, which has been in business since 1867, is more than just a meal, it's an experience. The menu never changes: Italian food served family-style on a plastic red-checked tablecloth — chicken $4, duck $5.75, steak $7.75, child's plate $2. The end of the meal is always the same, too: you leave the table carrying most of the "main course" in a paper bag for tomorrow's lunch. Dinner begins with sausage and cheese, a vinagrette bean salad, then a good thick soup, pickled cauliflower, a big green salad with chick peas and a loaf of sourdough with sweet butter, then ravioli or spaghetti, and finally, when you're thoroughly stuffed, half a roast chicken or duck served, along with crunchy potato slices, vegetables, a bowl of chicken gizzards in a delicious sauce and a plate of necks and backs in a spicy sauce. When you've given up, the waitress brings waxed paper and a bag. If you can manage it, there is rainbow sherbet or a warm banana fritter rolled in sugar for dessert. Remember that you must be famished when you arrive. Anything less won't be fair either to you or the cook.

Canoe Trips on the Russian River

W.C. "Bob" Trowbridge, 13849 Old Redwood Hwy. Tel. 433-4116, or 433-4103. $12.50 per canoe, 75¢ per person for life-jackets, $1 for car pick-up. Reservations, with 50 percent deposit, advisable in summer. For information on trips on the American River, Feather River, Sacramento River, Colorado River, Eel and Klamath Rivers, call 707-542-0598 or write to Box 942, Healdsburg, CA 95448.

● The picturesque, winding Russian River is perfect for family canoe trips. It's safe and very lovely but also fast enough to be exciting. Trowbridge opens its office at 8 every morning, and they like to have all boats in the water by noon. Asti Winery and the Alexander Bridge are the favored "heading out" places. Once you've reached your chosen destination, Trowbridge will provide a ride back to your car. On Saturday and Sunday

nights in summer, there are steak-and-beans-and-coleslaw barbecues at Healdsburg Beach for the perfect ending to your outing. Make sure everyone can swim!

Duncan Mills Depot Museum

3 miles from the ocean on Hwy. 116, Duncan Mills. Tel. 865-2573. Daily, 9 A.M.-5 P.M. Free.

● The only remaining depot of the North Pacific Coast Railroad, which ran the Sausalito-Cazadero route from 1877 to 1935, is now a small museum of railroad history. Photographs, tools, telegraph keys, bottles, and various memorabilia of the narrow-gauge passenger and logging railway may be seen in the depot — which is itself a museum piece. The depot stands at the entrance to the Duncan Mills campgrounds.

Fort Ross State Historic Park

Hwy. 1, 12 miles north of Jenner. Tel. Fort Ross 20. Museum: daily, 10 A.M.-5 P.M. $1 per car.

● Highway 1 goes right by Fort Ross. The old Russian Chapel recently burned down and is now restored, along with the rest of the Fort. Today visitors can climb to the top of the 8-sided blockade and the 7-sided blockade and look out over the little inlet, once a port for Russian fur traders. Part of the original fortifications, with a description of how it was built, still stands. Tools and equipment used by the fort's occupants since 1812 may be seen in the small museum in the Commodore's house, along with Russian samovar native plants, an Aleut kayak and artifacts found on the grounds.

Lake County Museum

175 3rd St. Lakeport. Tel. 263-5461, 1-4 P.M., Sat. 11 A.M.-4 P.M. Summer weekdays only. Free.

● This museum concentrates on Indian artifacts, particularly the arts and crafts of the Northern California Indians. A very good collection of Pomo baskets, feather polychrome baskets, a Tule boat, a rare rabbit blanket and arrowheads highlight the exhibit, and a display of pioneer equipment and furnishings is interesting.

The Farm Equipment Museum in the Fairgrounds displays a collection of well-used pioneer farm equipment. To see it, contact the Lake County Museum first.

Fort Ross

4

THE EAST BAY — ALAMEDA, CONTRA COSTA, AND SOLANO COUNTIES

The East Bay, ranging from the east shore of San Francisco Bay to Sacramento, is a green land dotted with public parks and streams, and crowned by Mt. Diablo. The places of interest in this area are some distance from each other, so it's advisable to plan ahead. The Berkeley hills across the bay from San Francisco, and the enchanting Delta to the east, frame the East Bay beautifully. Boaters, fishermen, picnickers, hikers and nature lovers of all ages will find special places to visit here.

Jack London Square

Foot of Broadway, Oakland.

● Busy waterfront stores and restaurants, the Oakland Convention Center and a constantly changing view of ships in the Oakland estuary make Jack London Square an interesting place for children to walk about. At one end of the square is a special treasure — The Jack London Klondike Cabin, a small, sod-covered cabin that housed Jack London in Yukon Territory during the Gold Rush in 1897. You'll see the crude furniture, rusty stove, shovels, snowshoes, gas lamps, pots and traps that Jack London used. You might want to pop into the First & Last Chance saloon nearby. Jack London is said to have imbibed

Biology Lab in the Lawrence Hall of Science

there — and the decor hasn't changed since then.

A few blocks away, the Bret Harte Boardwalk, a street of small frame shop buildings, is being restored to the way it looked in Gold Rush days. It's a romantic place to poke around.

Navy Marine Corps Museum

Building #1, Treasure Island. Tel. 781-1775. Daily, 10 A.M.-3:30 P.M. Free.

● An immense, 251' long bicentennial mural by artist Lowell Nesbitt portrays the history of Navy and Marine activities in the Pacific, in 11 historic events. Displays from the Mexican War of 1840 and the Boxer Rebellion of 1853 are of interest, along with collections of Navy and Marine historical artifacts, model ships and old uniforms.

Quinn's Lighthouse Restaurant

1951 Embarcadero, Oakland. Tel. 536-2050.

● The owners of San Francisco's Victoria Station restaurant believe in doing things right. When they want an English railroad atmosphere, they use real trains. And when they want a seafood place, they use a lighthouse, surrounded by water. Quinn's is a great two-story restaurant with glass walls, fine woods and hanging greenery.

Boats and water are on every side. Hearty sandwiches at lunchtime are served with barrels of peanuts in the shell. You can venture outside on the upper deck for closer views of the boats.

Dunsmuir House & Garden

2960 Peralta Oaks Court (106 Ave. exit on Hwy. 580). Sundays, noon-4 P.M., May-Oct. House tour $1, Garden tour 50¢.

● If you'd like to see the movie set for *Burnt Offerings*, and perhaps future Gothics, this is the place, minus a few cobwebs.

The Oakland Museum

1000 Oak St., Oakland. Tel. 273-3401. Tues.-Thurs. 10 A.M.-5 P.M.; Fri., to 10 P.M. Sat. 10 A.M.-5 P.M. Sun. 10 A.M.-6 P.M. Free. Free gallery tours on each level at 2 P.M. weekdays.

● The Oakland Museum is three first-rate museums in one: California art, California history, and California natural sciences. You can always be sure of finding an afternoon's worth of interesting things for children of all ages.

The top level concentrates on California art from the days of the Spanish explorers to the present. Panoramic views of San Francisco, cowboys and Indians, Oriental art found in California homes, and modern canvases are all amusing.

The natural sciences level includes exhibits on botany, birds, ecology, paleontology and geology.

An aquarium with everything from turkey fish to seahorses, plus dioramas of mammals, birds, rodents and snakes in their natural settings provide fascinating models of the real thing.

The California history level is perhaps the most intriguing of all. One begins with the Indians here in 3,000 B.C. and walks through "rooms" of the state's history, from the Spanish explorers, the Californios, the gold miners and wild west cowboys, to the pioneers and turn-of-the-century Californians. The pioneer kitchen is fascinating — with one chair of those grouped around the table actually outside the glass, so the young visitor can sit and pretend he's in the kitchen.

Concerts, films, and special exhibits on man and nature are scheduled regularly, and the snack bar is open daily until 3:30 P.M.

Oakland Zoo and Baby Zoo

Knowland State Park, MacArthur Freeway at Golf Links Rd. and 98th Ave., Oakland. Tel. 569-7353. Daily, 10 A.M.-5 P.M., weekends to 5:30 P.M., summer; 10 A.M.-4:30 P.M., weekends to 5 P.M. winter. 50¢ per car.
Baby Zoo: Tel. 569-8819. Daily, 10 A.M.-4:30 P.M. Adults, $1; over 65 and ages 2-14, 50¢. Rides, 20¢; train, 35¢.

● This beautifully arranged and landscaped zoo is one of the nicest in the state. The Jungle Lift can take you up over the African veldt, past the high ground where buffalo, deer and elk graze in a natural setting. A towering gibbon cage has a spiral walkway on which you can ascend all the way to the top to peek into the gibbon house. An elephant performs regularly.

In the Baby Zoo, children can feed and pet everything from baby lions, llamas and hippos, to pelicans, calves, seals, rabbits, swans, geese and ponies. There are chickens and baby chicks, even the baby chimps romp with their own play chairs. Kids can take turns riding the giant Galapagos turtle. Watch out for the goats — they eat anything, even mother's hem.

Children's Fairyland

Lakeside Park, Oakland. Tel. 832-3609. Daily, 10 A.M.-5:30 P.M., summer; Wed.-Sun., 10 A.M.-5:30 P.M., spring and fall; Sat., Sun., and holidays, 10 A.M.-4:30 P.M., winter. 50¢ for everyone.

● Duck through Mother Goose's Shoe to meet Alice, the Cheshire Cat, the Cowardly Lion and the Queen of Fairyland. Then slide down a dragon's back, listen to the Bong Tree that chimes when you step on the secret spots, or sail on a "pea green" boat with the Owl and the Pussycat. Pinocchio, Willie the Whale, slides, mazes, rides and enchanted bowers come to life. All of the characters in fairyland, from Humpty Dumpty to Mary's Little Lamb, are here to welcome children and make them smile. A magic key to unlock the stories is 50¢, Jolly Trolly train rides (25¢) and the Lakeside Park Toy Train (15¢), the Wonder-Go-Round is 10¢ and Magic Web Ferris Wheel is 25¢ and

Oakland Museum

seal food is 25¢. There are puppet shows and clown shows.

Lakeside Park

off Grand Ave., Oakland. Tel. 273-3296. Rotary Natural Science Center: Tel. 273-3739 Tues.-Sun., 10 A.M.-5 P.M. Free.

● A narrow strip of grass around Lake Merritt offers peace in the center of a busy city. In the Kiwanis Kiddie Korner of the park, children can swing on a sea horse or slide down an octopus. The outdoor aviary and zoo hold turkey vultures, barn owls, great horned owls, hawks and sand-hill cranes, along with opossums, porcupines, skunks, and other small animals. The Science Center shows free nature films on occasion, in addition to its regular fare of science exhibits. Lake Merritt is a wild duck refuge. For 15¢, you can buy duck food and feed the free flying waterfowl including an occasional pelican.

The Lakeside Toy Train runs from 12:30-5:30 P.M., depending on business. The round trip to Fairyland is 15¢ and takes 15 minutes.

Chabot Observatory & Planetarium

4917 Mountain Blvd. (near junction of MacArthur Freeway and Warren Blvd.), Oakland. Tel. 531-4560. Fri. and Sat., 7:30 P.M.; Adults, 50¢; children, 25¢. Reservations advised.

● The changing two-hour show here includes a movie, science demonstration, and the planetarium program. A recent show presented an exciting space voyage and observation through a large telescope at the different solar systems. Youngsters learn how astronomers explore the universe and get a chance to observe the planets and stars through a telescope. After finding out about the latest developments in astronomy, the audience adjourns for a little outdoor star gazing. Locating the Big and Little Dippers is always a popular part of the show with the budding astronomers in the crowd.

Meek Estate

Hampton & Boston Rds., Hayward. Tel. 581-6331. House: 8:30 A.M.-9:30 P.M.; Park: 8:30 A.M.-dusk. By appt. only.

● Lovers of Victoriana/nostalgia will love this totally furnished five-story 1869 national historic monument. Visitors can "pretend" in the ballroom, library, solarium, bedrooms, nursery, and servants' quarters.

There are acres of park and playground equipment for pent-up energies, and a barbecue in the picnic area.

Sulphur Creek Park

1801 'D' St., Hayward. Tel. 581-6331. Summer: Mon.-Sat., 10 A.M.-5 P.M.; Sun. noon-5 P.M. Winter closed. Fall, Spring; Mon.-Fri. 1-5 P.M.; Sat. 10 A.M.-5 P.M.; Sun. noon-5 P.M. Free.

• Sulphur Creek Park is a charming, out-of-the way spot in which to introduce children to nature. Ducks roam freely near the creek and rustic, outdoor cages hold hawks, foxes, raccoons, ringtailed cats, coatis, and opossum. Plants, trees, and fungus-bearing logs are neatly labelled throughout the grounds. The small museum is very education-oriented. There are touchable items, a question-and-answer exhibit on how snakes smell and birds eat, a display of the oddities of nature, rocks, minerals, seashells, a mock-up of life in a pond, and live and stuffed animals and reptiles. Local youngsters can take advantage of the animal lending library.

Mission San Jose

4330 Mission Blvd., Fremont. Tel. 656-9125. Daily, 10 A.M.-5 P.M. Free.

• Founded July 11, 1797, this mission is one of the smallest and least architecturally interesting of the California missions. However, the Mission San Jose has had an exciting place in California history. During the Gold Rush, it served as a trading post for miners, after surviving many years of Indian attacks. Father Duran, who arrived in 1806, taught some of the 2,000 Indian neophytes to play the original Mission bells and instruments now on display, along with timbers, rawhides and artifacts of the 1800s, a buggy, and vestments worn by Fra Serra. To get to the exhibits, visitors must push through a tapestry and enter the adobe living quarters of the mission padres. The olive grove planted in the gardens by the first padres still bears fruit.

Leslie Salt Company

7220 Central Ave., Newark. Tel. 797-1820. Tours Tues. and Thurs., 10:30 A.M., 1 and 3:30 P.M. by appt. (Children over 8 only). Free.

• See a film on how salt is harvested, refined and packaged, then tour the plant to see the pressing, packaging, carton-making, block pressing, and seasoning areas. It's an interesting industrial tour — and also an illuminating one. Did you know that salt is used not only to flavor food and soften water, but also to feed livestock, build roads, and drill oil wells?

East Bay Model Train Engineers Society

4075 Halleck St., Emeryville. Tel. 658-3537. Third Fri. of the month, 7:30-10 P.M.

• When you've gone through the caboose entrance you'll see the largest scale model railroad in the world — freight trains, steamliners, and more set up in their own special universe — well worth staying up late on one evening for.

The Campanile

Sather Tower, University of California, Berkeley. Tel. 642-6000. Daily, 10 A.M.-5 P.M. 10¢.

● A visit to the top of 307-foot Sather Tower, better known as the Campanile (after the famous bell towers of Renaissance Italy), would be a good place to start a tour of the Berkeley campus. An elevator running every 5 minutes takes you to the top of the tower, from which you can see San Francisco, Alcatraz, Mt. Tamalpais, both the Golden Gate and Bay bridges and the entire campus. A recorded message and a brochure tell you what you're looking at on each side. Above you, 12 bronze bells weighing almost 9 tons ring out a melody three times a day. The bells are played manually from inside the glass office in the middle of the viewing platform. Inside, and at the foot of the tower, are pictures of other famous towers of the world, memorabilia from the structure's sponsor, the Class of 1916, and a display of old timepieces and clocks.

University Art Museum

2626 Bancroft Way, Berkeley. Tel. 642-1207. Tues.-Sun., 11 A.M.-5 P.M. Free. Children's art festivals 3 times a year.

● Berkeley's new art museum is a natural for children — not so much because of the art, but because of the building itself. Its unique multileveled, concrete-slab construction enables a young visitor to see its spacious interiors from any of the many corners and balconies. The perspectives and viewpoints change constantly. The outdoor sculpture garden is fun and the primitive art usually finds a responsive audience in young people. The temporary exhibits are generally unusual and of interest, and there are often plays and concerts.

Large, bright Hans Hofmann paintings are on permanent display in the top gallery, and the many different kinds of futuristic chairs scattered around the galleries add to the fun.

The Pacific Film Archive, located downstairs in the museum (entrance at 2625 Durant Ave.; tel. 642-1412; 642-1124 for recorded message, daily; $1-$2.50 evenings; 75¢ matinees). A different film program every evening.

Lowie Museum

Kroeber Hall, University of California. (Bancroft & College Aves.), Berkeley. Tel. 642-3681. Mon.-Fri., 10 A.M.-4 P.M.; Sat. and Sun., noon-4 P.M. Adults, 25¢; children, 10¢.

● Across the street from the University Art Museum, a totem pole chronicles the family history of an Indian chief from the Queen Charlotte Islands and points the way to more anthropological treasures. The exhibits at Lowie change twice a year and are based upon the lifestyles and cultures of unusual peoples. Permanent exhibits include photographs of Ishi, the last of his tribe and plaster casts of Pleistocene Man. Also located in the building is

The Little Farm at Tilden Regional Park

the Worth Ryder Art Gallery, which frequently exhibits contemporary paintings and sculpture by students and faculty at the university.

Lawrence Hall of Science

Canyon Rd. North and Grizzly Peak Blvd. (east end of UC campus), Berkeley. Tel. 642-5132. Mon.-Fri., 10 A.M.-5 P.M. Thurs. evening til 9. Sat. and Sun., 10 A.M.-5 P.M. Adults $1; students, 75¢.

● Our 10- and 12-year-old nephews had to be dragged away from this place at closing time. There are almost too many exhibits — science workshops, tests of your mathematical and logical ability, tests of knowledge, computers to play with, visual oddities that help you learn more about how your eyes work, and a hundred different mechanical things to intrigue and amuse. The Biology Lab is the place to investigate the world of living things (weekends, 1-5). There is also an extensive mineral and gem collection and a grand view of the campus, the city and San Francisco Bay.

McCallum's Famous Ice Cream

1825 Solano, Berkeley. Tel. 525-3751. Daily, 7 A.M.-11 P.M. Fri. & Sat. til midnight.

● McCallum's specializes in delicious and mountainous ice cream creations. Try the hot fudge sundae, served with a pitcher of hot sauce and a cup of nuts on the side or the toasted almond chocolate shake in a tall glass lined with fudge. The McCallum Nightmare serves four to eight people from a tremendous silver platter 2 feet wide and a foot high. For $7.50, four to eight people get 24 shovels of twelve flavors of ice cream with fruit, butterscotch, hot fudge and many more toppings. Special sundaes range in price from $1 to $5.25 for the Hodge Podge that serves 3 to 6. Everything is dished out by Scotch-garbed lads and lassies, and there are cones on the other side of the store for on-the-run dining.

Tilden Regional Park & Environmental Education Center

Canyon Drive off Grizzly Peak Blvd., Berkeley Hills. Tel. 525-2233 Daily ex. Mon., 10 A.M.-5 P.M. Little Farm: Daily, 8 A.M.-5 P.M. Free.

● Tilden Park has a pony ride (35¢), a merry-go-round, a duck pond and a miniature train. Botanical gardens, a nature center and swimming in Lake Anza are some of the other recreational facilities in this well-equipped park. But the chief attraction of the park, especially for small children, is The Little Farm.

Mary Ann the Mexican burro, Snuffy the sheep, Rosebud the pig and Buttercup the cow are among the family members of this charming little farm. There are chickens, ducks and rabbits to feed and pet as well. Children are taught to walk toward the animals for petting and to feed them (with a flattened hand) only foods that are good for them.

Alexander Lindsay Junior Museum

1901 First Ave., Walnut Creek. Tel. 935-1978. Tues.-Fri., 1-5 P.M.; Sat., 10 A.M.-5 P.M. Free.

• A miniature zoo housing touchable animals and birds, an aquarium of native fish and amphibians and a collection of rocks, fossils, shells and Indian artifacts are the main features of this small museum. Coyotes, badgers, foxes, owls, hawks, skunks and snakes are a few of the animals on display. Some of the smaller domestic animals can be rented for $1 a year.

Diablo Valley College Museum & Planetarium

321 Golf Club Rd., Pleasant Hill. Tel. 685-1230, ext. 303. Museum: Mon., Wed., Fri., 9:30 A.M.-noon, 1-4:30 P.M. Sat., 1:30-5 P.M. (closed Sats. in August). Planetarium shows: Sat., 3 P.M. Group shows at 1 P.M. Free.

• Youngsters will be attracted to this college museum. Here, they can watch a seismograph work, see a Foucault pendulum swing, study the changing anthropological exhibits on Native Americans and see an oceanography exhibit depicting sea and shore life, mollusks, tidepools and navigation tests. During our visit we saw a very interesting exhibit on fossils. Local animals and edible plants are on display, as are a few alien animals (Norway rats, pheasants) and a special exhibit of nocturnal creatures such as moles, weasels and owls. The planetarium's astronomy programs are always fun.

Muriel's Doll House Museum

33 Canyon Lake Drive, Port Costa. Tel. 787-2820. Daily ex. Mon., 10 A.M.-7 P.M. Adults, $1; children, 25¢.

• Muriel greets you at the door leaning on a peppermint-striped glass cane. After you sign her guest book, you may browse through her collection of China, bisque, Parian, wood wax, apple, tin, celluloid and fashion dolls reflecting the customs and costumes of their respective eras. There are Indian dolls, Eskimo dolls, Amish dolls, black dolls, and cornhusk, papier-maché, and rag dolls. Antique toys, books and doll houses are also on display. For a unique experience, look into several "shadow box" scenes from Dickens' *Great Expectations*, an 1886 moonshiner's still and a 1900 barber shop. For history buffs, there are Mary Todd and Abraham Lincoln dolls, 17th-century Italian creche dolls and Sarah Bernhardt dolls. Muriel's Doll House is a fun side trip for all doll lovers, and Muriel, who loves to tell intriguing stories about the dolls, will greatly enhance the experience.

Muriel's Doll House Museum

65

John Muir National Historic Site

John Muir National Historic Site

4202 Alhambra Ave., Martinez. Tel. 228-4330. Tours daily on the hour 10-11 A.M., 1-4 P.M. 50¢.

● After a beautiful half-hour film of John Muir's words and the natural wonders that inspired them, visitors may take a self-guiding tour through Muir's large 19th-century farmhouse, which is one of the most authentically presented houses you can visit. Details like closets filled with clothing, Muir's suitcase on the bed ready for travel and the glasses and pencils, books and papers standing ready for use on Muir's desk in his study or "scribble den," give the house a genuine lived-in look. You can go up to the treasure-filled attic, from which Muir used to shout orders to his farmhands.

Also on the Muir property is the Martinez Adobe (open Sat. and Sun. afternoons) which was built by the son of the Mexican don who built the town of Martinez. The thick-walled adobe has served as headquarters for the Rancho foreman's quarters on the Muir Ranch, and home for Muir's daughter and family. You may wander through the gounds and look at the exotic plants Muir gathered for as long as you like.

Benicia Capitol State Historic Park

1st and G Streets, Benicia. Tel. 745-3385. Daily, 10 A.M.-5 P.M. Adult ticket, 25¢, usable at all state parks that day.

● Benicia was the capitol of California for over a year. This red brick building has since served as a courthouse, church, school, jail, community hall, firehouse, police station, museum, theater and library. Today it's restored to its appearance as the state capitol building of 1854. The Assembly room, the Senate Chamber, and the committee rooms are completely reconstructed and furnished with fine old desks, legislative ledgers, whale oil lamps, quill pens and shiny brass cuspidors. The exhibit room provides the history about the days of early California and the ranger can tell you even more. Most 4th graders in the area have been here and enjoyed the visit.

Across the colorful garden is the *Joseph Fischer Home*, which will be open to the public as soon as the foundations are repaired.

The Nut Tree Restaurant

The Nut Tree Restaurant

Nut Tree Rd. off Hwy. 80, Vacaville, Tel. 448-6411. Daily, 7 A.M.-9 P.M.

● The highway signs for the Nut Tree are so pretty you wonder if the restaurant can live up to them. It does. The Nut Tree is much more than a restaurant — it's an afternoon of enjoyment. The restaurant itself is three beautifully decorated rooms facing huge glass aviaries where brilliantly colored birds fly, sing and eat fruits and seeds. The luncheon menu includes salads, sandwiches and special lunches ranging in price from $3. Every diner gets an individual loaf of warm bread. The din-ner menu is more; the turkey tamale plate, for example, is $6.35 at dinner (half that at lunch). You can order a Dutch plate of cold meats and cheese or a splendiferous fresh fruit plate ($4.65 at dinner, less at lunch). Beer is imported from thirteen countries and the desserts are divine. Children under 10 rate a special Train Rider's menu of fruit, soup, baby food, chicken, prawns, burgers or peanut butter — with fries and appropriate condiments and all under $3. Aside from the main restaurant, there's a nice cheese and beer place, an outside snack bar and a pocketbook-boggling gift shop to spend hours in. And don't worry about the kids —

they can spend hours on the free mechanical animals in front of the play mirrors and funnyface houses, or inside the Polynesian tree huts. They can also see a a puppet show, explore a fantastic toy store or take a 5-minute miniature train ride (35¢) that goes through a tunnel and past the airport (where they can take a plane ride for $5 adults, $3 children). All this sprung from a single walnut carried by a 12-year-old Iowa girl in 1860!

The Pena Adobe

5 miles south of Vacaville on Hwy. 80, Pena Adobe Rd. Tel. 448-6262 ext. 36. Hours still uncertain.

● The Penas and the Vacas were the first Mexican settlers in this area and the Pena adobe is the original one built on an ancient Indian site in the days of the ranchos. It still contains some of the original furnishings and many Wintu Indian artifacts which were found during the restoration. The spool bed and spinning wheel in the bedroom are excellent examples of pioneer craft and the saddles in the bunk room are authentically worn-out.

California Railway Museum

Hwy. 12, Rio Vista Junction, Tel. 374-2978. Weekends and holidays 12-5 P.M. Free. Street car rides on Sun.; Adults, $1; children 50¢ all day.

● The California Railway Museum was restored by the non-profit organization of men who love trains. You can walk through and around the 65 retired trolleys and steam locomotives or just watch the railroad buffs at work renovating the collection. The children's favorites were the electric freight locomotives, an Indian passenger car and an old-fashioned Salt Lake & Utah observation coach. They also climbed over an electric cable car, a N.Y.C. "el" car, a Birney Street "dinkey" (a 5¢ street car) a "Boat" car from Blackpool, England, a real Toonerville from the Key system, and a nice old Sutter Street cable car. The gift shop at the entrance to the yard is equally nostalgic; you can find photos, books, model kits, tickets, badges and even old ads from street cars and trains. An operating electric railroad meanders through the property. Picnic lawn available.

Public Relations Tours

The Factory

1906 Broadway, Alameda. Tel. 522-3353. Shops open 10 A.M.-10 P.M. daily; Restaurant open 11 A.M.-4 P.M. daily.

● Saturday morning puppet shows and a huge stained glass whale hang-

ing from the ceiling entrance children of all ages in this craft shop complex. Potters, weavers, quilters and macrame-makers offer demonstrations and classes, along with wares. The book store has a large selection of children's books. The restaurant specializes in cheese and chocolate fondues.

A/C Transit

1140 45th St., Emeryville. Tel. 654-7878, ext. 311, 312, 313. Free tours (by appt.) weekdays 10 A.M.-2 P.M. (children over 6 only).

• See the work it takes to keep the buses rolling; ride a bus through the automatic bus washer.

Kilpatrick's Bakeries, Inc.

955 Kennedy, Oakland. Tel. 534-3600. Free tours by appt. Mon. & Fri. noon-4 P.M.; Thurs. 1-4 P.M.

• See how bread is baked and packaged.

Paramount Theatre of the Arts

2025 Broadway, Oakland. Tel. 465-6400. Tours by appt.

• The Paramount, which has regular programs of interest to children, is the best example of "Art Deco" architecture on the West Coast. Parquet floors, a gold ceiling teaming with sculptured life and elegant 30's embellishments almost compete with what's on stage.

Gin Shing Bakery & Fortune Cookie Factory

378 9th Street, bet. Franklin & Webster Sts., Oakland. Tel. 832-5552. Mon.-Sat. 10 A.M.-3 P.M. by appt. only for ages 6 & up. Free.

• If you've ever wanted to write your own fortune, here's your chance. For 5¢, you can bring with you a fortune of your own devising, typed or written on a piece of paper no larger than ½" x 2½". It will be returned to you in short order inside a fortune cookie. A 10-15 minute tour shows how fortune cookies are made. An understandably popular stop with smart cookies everywhere. School groups welcome.

D'Lar Candle Co.

600 Hoffman St., Richmond. Tel. 236-0442. Tours, 30-45 minutes long, by appt. 25¢

• See candles of all shapes and sizes being made — and make one of your own to take home.

Tri-Valley Herald

2277 Third St., Livermore. Tel. 447-2111. Mon.-Fri., 10 A.M.-4 P.M. Free.

• This small (circulation 10,000) daily newspaper welcomes occasional visitors who'd like to learn how a newspaper is put together. The printing is done at night, so you can just see the writers writing, editors editing, artists pasting up layouts and advertising men calling businesses. Mornings are best for casual drop-in visits, but it's always good to call for an appointment.

Winchester Mystery House

5

THE PENINSULA AND THE SAN JOSE AREA

The Peninsula and the San Jose area can provide many days of happy "attraction" hunting. There are huge amusement parks, such as Frontierland and Marine World/Africa U.S.A., small museums, lovely parks, interesting industries. A map showing city streets is helpful, and it might be a good idea to map out your day, before you set out. Fast foods places flourish on all of the roads here, and picnic areas are always close by, so impromptu meals are easy.

Rod McLellan Orchidary

1450 El Camino Real, South San Francisco, Tel. 871-5655. Greenhouses and shops open daily, 8 A.M.-5 P.M. Free guided tours, 10:30 A.M. and 1:30 P.M.

● The heavenly smell of acres of orchids hits you the minute you enter the Rod McLellan orchidary. A guide shows you to the greenhouse where the flowers are pollinated by hand and then incubated until they sprout. Lessons in modern techniques of hybridizing and caring for house plants are given. In rear greenhouses, you'll see roses, spiral eucalyptus, gardenias and stephanotis, but the memory the whole family will bring away with them is orchids in more colors, types and sizes than anyone could dream existed.

The Sanchez Adobe

Linda Mar Blvd., Pacifica. Tel. 359-1881. Wed.-Sun., 10 A.M.-noon, 1-4 P.M. Free.

● The Sanchez Adobe, once the home of the *Alcalde* (mayor) of San Francisco, is now a small museum of 19th-century furnishings and artifacts. Baby shoes, parasols, carbon and gas irons, wool carding tools, foot warmers, Harper's Weeklys, an 1853 edition of Shakespeare are mingled with mementos of the Sanchez family. The furnishings in an upstairs parlor and bedroom are spare and simple, with a very realistic mixture of Victorian and Rancho styles. The Sanchez Adobe is historically important as the center of the Mission Dolores rancho and as the site of the earliest Spanish settlement in San Mateo County.

Coyote Point Museum

For Environmental Education Coyote Point Park, San Mateo. Tel. 573-2595. Mon.-Sat., 9 A.M.-5 P.M.; Sun., 1-5 P.M. Free.

● This small, nicely arranged museum covers all aspects of the natural history of San Mateo. Rock formations, shells from Coyote Point, coastal animals, bayshore birds and dioramas of chaparral and redwood wildlife are some features of the exhibit. The children were especially interested in the local fossils, the live tortoises, lizards and geckos, the skeleton of a horse and an exhibit on natural camouflage in birds, fish, insects and butterflies.

The picnic grounds nearby are always cool.

Japanese Tea Garden

Central Park, San Mateo. Tel. 347-5266. Mon.-Fri., 8 A.M.-4 P.M.; Sat. and Sun., 11 A.M.-5 P.M. Free tours and lectures in summer, daily 11 A.M.-4 P.M.

● This proper, gracious Japanese garden is a soothing spot in the midst of city bustle. Quaint bridges and rock pathways take the visitor past a waterfall, a pond thick with waterlilies and goldfish and, in the springtime, the delicate cherry blossoms. In the summer, the teahouse is open and geishas explain Japanese customs. Occasional demonstrations of the meticulously choreographed tea ceremony are fascinating for all ages.

San Mateo County Historical Museum

1700 W. Hillsdale Blvd., San Mateo. Tel. 574-6441. Mon.-Fri., 9:30 A.M.-4:30 P.M.; Sat., 10:30 A.M.-4:30 P.M. Free.

● A walk through this museum is a walk through history. You begin with the Pleistocene Period — 14 million years ago — and view the plants, bones and fossils found in San Mateo from that age. Then to the period of man in San Mateo, 3,000 years ago, when the Costanoan Indians began to leave evidence of their lifestyle. You see a skeleton and a diorama of a village, along with descriptions of their magic dances, boats, tools and food. The Mission and Rancho periods are well-represented and the pioneer period includes an exhibit of lumber mills, the old general store and bar, settlers' wagons, unicycles and memorabilia from the 19th century. Although the collection is not very extensive, what this museum does have is very well presented.

SFO Helicopter

TWA Gate 53, San Francisco International Airport. Tel. 626-7700. Thirteen times a day. $6.48.

● Cruise up to Marin, fly over to the East Bay and return to San Francisco International after a wondrous forty-five minute flight. Seats for the round-trip tour are sold on a stand-by basis only — but you can always watch planes taking off and landing while you wait.

Japanese Tea Garden, San Mateo

Farrell's Ice Cream Parlour

109 Bovet Rd., San Mateo. Tel. 345-1894. Sun.-Thurs., 11:30 A.M.-11 P.M.; Fri. and Sat., to 1 A.M.

● Farrell's brings all of a child's fantasies to life in its birthday extravaganzas. Birthdays are celebrated with drums, whistles, bells, candles and the entire restaurant singing to the birthday child. The Birthday Party package ($1.65 each) includes soft drinks, favors, gifts and surprises for at least ten kids, plus the fabulous Zoo sundae: eight ice creams, five sherbets, five toppings and almonds, whipped cream, cherries and bananas (sundae alone-$8.50). Other Farrell's specialties start at 95¢ for an old-fashioned sundae, soda or shake (soda water is still 2¢ plain) and "end" with the $2 Pig's Trough sundae (there's a special award if you finish this one by yourself). If you're not in the mood for ice cream, Farrell's offers old-time sandwiches, from peanut butter and jelly to hamburgers to the Gastronomical- Delicatessen-Epicurian's Delight — a loaf of French bread piled with enough meat and cheese to feed four hungry people for $6.95.

There are other Farrell's in Sunnyvale, San Jose, Fremont, Sacramento, Hayward, Fresno, and Serramonte in Daly City.

Pigeon Point Lighthouse

5½ miles south of Pescadero, Pigeon Point, San Mateo Co. 1-4 P.M. summer weekends. Free.

● Rock and sandstone bluffs have created fascinating tidepools to gaze into while you walk this curve of beach and visit the tiny lighthouse.

Marine World/Africa USA

Marine World Parkway (Ralston Ave.) off Bayshore Freeway, Redwood City. Tel. 591-7676. Daily, 9:30 A.M.-6:30 P.M., Apr.-Sept.; Sept. & Oct.: Wed.-Fri. 9:30 A.M.-5:30 P.M., til 6:30 on weekends; weekends only, Nov.-Mar. Adults, $5.25; ages 5-12, $3.25.

● Marine World/Africa USA is as advertised, really wild. Although the price may seem high, you'll find that the family can spend the entire day there happily — and not pay for anything else except food (which you can bring yourself). Shows are scheduled so you can go from one to another at an easy pace. You will watch trained whales and jungle cats perform, cheer the Dolphin Olympics, take a river raft past giraffes, baboons and white rhinos, walk through an underwater aquarium, pet a porpoise or an aoudad, see a water-ski show, ride a camel, giggle at puppet shows, wander through a fun-filled jungle and finally, relax on a boat ride. It's all fun — for all ages.

Sunset Magazine

Middlefield and Willow Rds., Menlo Park. Tel. 321-3600. Free tours: Mon.-Fri., 10:30 and 11:30 A.M., 1, 2 and 3 P.M. Gardens open 9 A.M.-4:30 P.M.

● Cliff May designed the Sunset

Birthday Party at Farrell's Ice Cream Parlor

buildings to give the staff a clear view of the famous gardens and, at the same time, to prevent uncomfortable glare. The buildings and gardens are some of the most beautiful to be found in a business environment. The garden itself is what children like best: they can walk from one end to the other and view, in order, the botanical life of the western coast of America — the desert plants of Baja, the cactus of Southern California, the coastal shrubs of Monterey, the rhododendrons and sturdy trees of Oregon and Washington. Older youngsters with an interest in journalism will enjoy the office tour. If they have the idea that working on a magazine is all glamor, they may change their minds after visiting the busy advertising, editorial and test-kitchen offices.

West Bay Model Railroad Club

1090 Merrill St., Menlo Park. Tel. 323-3898. 3rd Fri. and 4th Wed. of month, 8-10 P.M. Free.

● Three different-sized trains run on the club's 4,000 feet of track, whistling past miniature towns and painted scenery and over tiny bridges and turntables. Adding to the effectiveness of the show is a tape of special sound effects interspersed with the story of how the club came about. The club also has a railroad-stationary display, a library and a machine shop. The members' special Christmas show on a December weekend is a favorite event for local youngsters.

Baylands Nature Interpretive Center

2775 Embarcadero Rd., Palo Alto. Tel. 329-2506. Mon.-Fri., 2-5 P.M.; Sat. and Sun., 10 A.M.-5 P.M. Free.

● Owned and run by the city of Palo Alto, this bayside nature center is on a boardwalk adjacent to a salt marsh. The Center focuses on the conservation, ecology and natural history of the Bay Area. Pictures of local birds, a plant exhibit, a saltwater aquarium and various changing displays are open throughout the week. The weekend, however, is the best time to bring the children, for the regular exhibits are supplemented by nature movies at 11 A.M. and 4 P.M., slide lectures at 1 P.M. and nature walks in the marsh at 2 P.M. and an open ecology workshop at 3 P.M.

Palo Alto Junior Museum & Zoo

Rinconada Park (1451 Middlefield Rd.), Palo Alto. Tel. 329-2111. Tues.-Fri., 10 A.M.-5 P.M.; Sat., 10 A.M.-5 P.M.; Sun. and holidays, 1-4 P.M. Free.

Animal demonstrations on Saturdays at 11:15 A.M. and 2:15 P.M., and the daily feeding time is 3:30 P.M.

● This beautifully constructed museum has constantly changing exhibits to keep kids coming back for more. The permanent collection includes a large camera obscura, fossils, nests, and Native American artifacts. Outside, in the poured concrete shelters, there are snakes and reptiles, bobcats, ravens, squirrels and lovable rabbits. Ducks nest under the bridge that curves over the pretty duck pond. An aquarium is now being built.

Stanford University

Stanford. Tel. 497-2300. Free tours of campus start Mon.-Fri. at 11 A.M. and 2:15 P.M. from Memorial Court. Stanford Guide Service, Hoover Institution Lobby (497-2053) Mon.-Fri., 8 A.M.-5 P.M.; Sat. 8:30 A.M.-1 P.M.; Sun. 1-4 P.M. Free tours of Stanford Linear Accelerator Center by appt. Tel. 854-3300 ext. 2204.

Hoover Institution on War, Revolution & Peace

Stanford University, Tel. 497-2053. Mon.-Fri. 8 A.M.-5 P.M. Free. Observation Platform, 25¢, Mon.-Fri. 11 A.M.-noon, 1-4 P.M.; Sat., 1-4 P.M. 10 A.M.-noon; Sun, 1-4 P.M.

● In addition to the lovely view from its tower, the Hoover Institution offers memorabilia of Herbert Hoover, a Stanford alumnus. Older children should enjoy the pictures, cartoons, diaries, honors, furnishings and other mementos from Hoover's White House years and world crusades. A settee and chairs that belonged to Abraham Lincoln are also on view.

Leland Stanford, Jr., Museum

Stanford University. Tel. 497-4177. Tues.-Fri., 10 A.M.-5 P.M., Sat. and Sun., 1-5 P.M. Free.

● Remembrances of the Stanford Family are displayed in this luxurious building, along with a widely varied collection of Indian artifacts, fine and primitive art and sculpture, a jade collection, and an Egyptorium (with a mummy in an open case). The Stanford Rooms feature toy trains and soldiers, a check signed by George Washington in 1799, family portraits, children's books, old weapons, archaeological findings from Pompeii, and Mrs. Stanford's gowns. If you look carefully, you'll also find the original "Gold Spike" driven in 1869 to complete the nation's first transcontinental railroad.

Marriott's Great America

No. 1 Great American Pkwy off Bayshore Freeway, Santa Clara. Tel. 988-1776. Weekends, 3/20-5/29 and 9/7-10/30; 10-10 Daily in summer and Easter vacation. Adults, $7.95; ages 4-11 $6.95 (admission + all rides + entertainment).

● This 200-acre family entertainment center, scheduled to open in March, 1976, aims to out-Disney Disneyland. Families can wander from Hometown Square of the 1920's thru a turn-of-the-century County Fair, to the Yukon Territory, Orleans Place and Yankee Harbor, a 19th century New England Fishing Village. There are 28 restaurants, all themed with employees in costumes, 30 shops and boutiques, 27 rides and five theaters featuring everything from a "Broadway" revue to a live animal show. Something for everyone?

Campbell Rock Shop and Museum

*412 E. Campbell Ave., Campbell.
Tel. 378-6935. Tues., Fri., Sat., 10
A.M.-5:30 P.M.; Wed. & Thur. 10 A.M.-9
P.M. Free.*

● Over 1,000 different types of gems and minerals from all over California and the world are displayed in the shop and more formally in the museum. Narcasite, marmatite, malachite, opals, garnets, tourmaline, calcite, agates, quartz crystal and rose quartz are shown in rough, cut and polished stones. A fluorescent-rock exhibit is fun under black light, and the back of the store is a wonderful jumble of rough-cut gems piled in baskets and cases. Jewelry-making and lapidary classes are given throughout the year, for both children and adults.

Mission Santa Clara de Asis

*University of Santa Clara, The
Alameda, 820 Alviso, Santa Clara.
Tel. 984-4242. Daily, 6 A.M.-8 P.M.,
summer; 6 A.M.-10:30 P.M. during
school terms. Free.*

● Founded in 1777 and today part of the university campus, the present mission is a replica of the third building raised on this site by the mission fathers. An adobe wall from the original cloister still stands in the peaceful garden. The original cross of the mission stands in front of the church, and the bell given by the King of Spain in 1778 still tolls. Visit the deSaisset Gallery and Ricard Observatory and California Environmental Gallery with artifacts dating to 1777.

Hakone Japanese Gardens

*21000 Big Basin Way, Saratoga. Tel.
867-3438. Daily, 10 A.M.-5 P.M.; closed
holidays. Teahouse and gift shop:
10:30 A.M.-5 P.M., May-Oct. Free.*

● Walk along curving, foliage-lined paths, through a wisteria-covered arbor, step on 3 stones to get across a stream next to 3 waterfalls. Climb a moon bridge to see the goldfish. Discover little houses and gazebos hidden in the trees. Spy stone and wooden lanterns, statues of cranes and cats hidden in the foliage. Rest in a peaceful, tatami-matted teahouse overlooking shaped trees and bushes. Sit in a wisteria-roofed summerhouse. This wonderful garden was designed by a former court gardener to the Emperor of Japan as a hill and water garden, the strolling pond style typical of Zen gardens in the 17th century. Walking here, you might be transported to any century but the hustling 20th.

Engine House

*672 Alberta, nr. Hollenbach & Fremont, Sunnyvale. Tel. 245-0609.
Wed. & Thurs., noon-6 P.M.; Fri.,
noon-9 P.M.; Sat., 10 A.M.-6 P.M.; Sun.,
noon-9 P.M., longer in summer and
before Christmas.*

● One million items ("the next million we have on order") of interest to train fans are crammed into this treasure-filled space. Cars, kits, photos, hobby magazines, models of trains from old wood-burners to BART, and everything you'd need to create a complete train world can be found in this, the largest train shop in the West. A museum is in the works.

Villa Montalvo

Saratoga – Los Gatos Road, Saratoga. Tel. 867-3421. Arboretum: Daily, 8 A.M.-5 P.M. Galleries: daily ex. Mon., 1-4 P.M. 25¢.

● Nature trails traverse a redwood grove, hills and meadows, and flower-covered arbors in this county-run arboretum. The villa's grounds are also a bird sanctuary and as many as 41 species of birds may be spotted in a single day. The villa takes its name from a 16th-century novel written by Montalvo, a Spanish author. The story describes a tribe of Amazons living in a fabulous island paradise named California! The Amazons rode on gryphons, and the many stone gryphons on the grounds are sure to entrance youngsters. This palatial former home of the late U.S. senator and San Francisco mayor, James D. Phelan, is now a center for young artists, whose works are shown in the galleries.

Billy Jones Wildcat Railroad

Oak Meadow Park, Los Gatos. Tel. 354-8320. Summer: Daily ex. Mon. 11 A.M.-5:30 P.M., Sun. from noon. Spring and Fall: Sat. 11 A.M.-5:30 P.M., Sun. noon-5:30 P.M. Adults, 50¢; under 16, 25¢.

● A full steam narrow-gauge, 18-inch prairie-type railroad toots along a mile long track pulling four open cars seating 30 people each. The short ride takes you into the forest, near a stream, and back to the bustling city park.

Los Gatos Museum

Tait and Main Sts., Los Gatos. Tel. 354-2646. Daily, 1-4 P.M.; Sun., 2-4 P.M. Free.

● The art section of this welcoming museum features constantly changing historical and contemporary art exhibits. The natural history room has a fluorescent minerals exhibit and a table where you can touch petrified wood, talc, Indian mortars and a fossil whale vertebra. It also features Paiute Indian artifacts, seashells, birds, nests and reptiles, but these exhibits, normally fascinating to children, will take second place to the beehive. A glass cage surrounds this thriving hive on all sides but the outer wall and you can stand for hours watching the bees fly in and out, filling and eating their honey comb. If you're very quiet, you can even hear them singing.

Foothill College Planetarium & Observatory

1234 El Monte Rd., Los Altos Hills. Tel. 948-8590, ext. 381. Planetarium: Fri., 7:15 and 8:30 P.M., Oct.-May. Adults, $1; students and senior citizens, 75¢; under 12, 50¢. Observatory: Summer (starting June 19): Mon.-Fri., dusk until 10:30 P.M.; summer; Fri., dusk until 10:30 P.M., and Sat. (if clear), 9 A.M.-noon and dusk until 10:30 P.M., winter. Free.

Frontier Village

● Every Friday night during the school year, the planetarium puts on hour science spectaculars, using exciting special effects to take visitors on space trips to the Milky Way and to other planets and stars. The observatory offers a slide show on space, a 16½-inch reflector to examine and several small telescopes for looking at the stars. The Forum building on the Foothill campus presents free science films during the school year on Fridays at 7:30 P.M. The programs, which are always interesting for older children, change monthly. A space science museum is scheduled to open later in 1973.

Foothill College Electronics Museum

1234 El Monte Rd. Los Altos Hills. Tel. 948-8590. Wed. & Thurs. 9 A.M.-5 P.M. Fri. 9 A.M.-10 P.M. Sat. & Sun. 1-5 P.M. Free.

● The most complete collection of ancient radio tubes, spark transmitters and klytrons in the world is now open to radio hobbyists of all ages. Special exhibits that allow visitors to experiment with tubes, transmitters and receivers are most popular.

Minolta Planetarium

De Anza College, 21250 Stevens Creek Blvd., Cupertino. Tel. 257-5550. Thurs. & Fri. 4 and 8 P.M.; Sat. & Sun., 3 & 8 P.M.; Adults, $1.50, Students and senior citizens, $1; under 12, 75¢.

● The Minolta Planetarium employs the latest audio-visual equipment and techniques to present a remarkable show. The main projector spreads the night sky across a 50-foot dome, and a total of 24 sound speakers and 150 other projectors are used to produce some "far-out" effects. These mechanical marvels take you not only through space but through time: you fly to the moon to look at the brilliance of the stars *sans* pollution, as they were seen by the astronauts, then you travel back in time to see how the stars looked when man first saw them. It's a wondrous experience that truly combines education and entertainment. The new Environmental Study Area, open from noon-4 P.M. the 1st Sat. of each month & by appt., provides a variety of biological environments representing major communities in California.

Frontier Village

4885 Monterey Rd. (Hwy. 82), San Jose. Tel. 225-1500. Winter, weekends & holidays, 10 A.M.-5 P.M.; Summer: Mon.-Thurs., 10 A.M.-5 P.M., Fri. & Sat. 10 A.M.-10 P.M.; Sun. 10 A.M.-7 P.M. Adults $3.25, children $2.75. Admission & all rides ticket, $4.50.

● The family will have a great, fun-filled day at this Western amusement park. You can ride a stagecoach, or take a pack train, try your hand at trout fishing, visit Indian dwellings and an 1890's schoolhouse, canoe through "Indian territory." Noisy gunfights and bank robberies are staged without warning; keep the little ones in hand so they won't be alarmed at the sudden tumult. The young children will particularly enjoy the Petting Island with lots of small, cuddly animals. For the whole family, there are regularly scheduled Wild West shows and a saloon that serves up ice cream, sarsaparilla and Dixieland music. Picnic spots are available if you bring your own lunch.

Japanese Friendship Tea Garden

1490 Senter Rd., San Jose. Tel. 294-4706. Tues.-Fri., 11 A.M.-5 P.M.; Sat. and Sun., to 5:30 P.M. (closing time extended to sunset in summer). Free.

● This lovely Japanese garden is patterned after the Korakuen garden in San Jose's sister city of Okayama. The three lakes are designed to symbolize the word "kokoro," which means heart, mind and soul. Picturesque bridges and waterfalls, shaped rocks and trees, and land and water flowers are wonderful to walk through. The Teahouse is open until sunset for traditional Japanese luncheons, tea and cookies (45¢) and lovely gifts. You can also buy fish food here to feed the magnificent golden carp.

Happy Hollow Park & Baby Zoo

Kelley Park, Keyes and Senter Rds., San Jose. Tel. 292-8188. Daily, 10 A.M.-4 P.M. Ages 15-80, $1; 2-14, 60¢.

● A miniature Viking ship, gingerbread house and King Arthur's castle are some of the attractions of this delightful children's park along with the Old Mill, the Crooked House, Alice in Mirrorland and the Haunted House. There are places to climb, things to ride and animals to pet, including deer and seals that do tricks for you. Free puppet shows are at 12, 2 and 4 P.M. Or you can ride on Danny the Dragon, a paddle wheel boat and a pretty merry-go-round. The Baby Zoo is inhabited by lions, tigers, hippos, elephants, chimpanzees and seals. King Neptune's carousel is fun and you can ride the Safari Shuttle to the Museum.

San Jose Historical Museum

Kelley Park, 635 Phelan Ave., San Jose. Tel. 287-2290. Mon.-Fri., 10 A.M.-4:30 P.M.; Sat. and Sun., noon-4:30 P.M. Family group, 50¢, adult, 25¢; ages 8-17, 10¢.

● Eight rooms tell the history of Santa Clara Valley, from the first people, the Ohlone Indians, through the Spanish and Mexican rancheros and vaqueros and the Yankee pioneers. The New Almaden Mine Room displays artifacts from the first quicksilver mine in North America, including a slanted, narrow ladder used in the mine.

The children will particularly enjoy an 1885 nickelodeon, a 5¢ movie of the San Francisco earthquake, firefighting equipment and a 19th-century school room furnished with an early teacher's double desk, a "regulator" clock, and a blackboard.

San Jose Zoo

San Jose City Park, Keyes and Senter Rd., San Jose. Tel. 293-2229. Mon.-Sat. 10 A.M.-4 P.M., Sun. 11 A.M.-5 P.M. Adults, $1; children, 60¢.

● If you're visiting this beautifully landscaped zoo near closing time, the children will learn what all the animals eat. Who could have guessed that the cassowary bird from Australia eats strawberries and bananas? Malaysian otters, anteaters, baby sun bears, pelicans, fur seals in a private sand-surrounded pond and a sleepy sloth are among the many animals to see. Be sure to see the False Gavials, mother and daughter, strange, gold-colored crocodiles in their cubicles. At certain times you can look into the under-the-river observation area to watch otters and other river creatures living undisturbed by people.

Rosicrucian Egyptian Museum, Science Museum, & Planetarium

Rosicrucian Park, Naglee and Park Aves., San Jose. Tel. 287-9171. Egyptian Museum: Tues.-Fri., 9 A.M.-5 P.M.; Sat.-Mon., noon-5 P.M.; Free. Science Museum: Wed.-Sun., 1-5 P.M., summer; weekends only,

Happy Hollow Children's Park

winter. Free. Planetarium: weekends only, 1-5 P.M., with hourly shows. Adult, $1; ages 6 to 16, 50¢.

• The wondrous, faraway world of ancient Egypt awaits you and your children in this museum — the most extensive Egyptian and Babylonian collection we've seen in America. Mummies, sculpture, paintings, jewelry, cosmetics, scarabs, scrolls, and amulets are found here in abundance. One room concentrates on mummies, both human and animal, and funereal objects. The ornate coffins, mummified cats and falcons, toys that were buried with children, and descriptions of the embalming process are totally absorbing. Our four-year-old kept wanting to know how old everybody was. A short tour takes you inside a rock tomb, through the outer hallways and into the crypt to see wall paintings, false doorways, and the sarcophagus itself. Another level of the museum shows modern art and 18th-century French furniture.

Next door is the Science Museum and Planetarium. The Science Museum houses a series of exhibits that demonstrate the laws of physical science. There are lots of buttons to push, and you can see your voice patterns and observe a seismograph and moon model. The planetarium show changes monthly.

Winchester Mystery House

525 South Winchester Blvd., San Jose. Tel. 247-2000. Daily, 9 A.M.-6 P.M., summer; to 4:30 P.M. winter. House & Grounds tour. Adults, $4.25; ages 5-12, $2.75. House Tour, Adults, $3.50, children, $2. Both tour inc. museum. Museum only: Adults, $1; children, 75¢.

• Sarah Winchester, widow of the Winchester Rifle heir, was told by a gypsy that as long as she kept building something, she would never die. This house is a monument to 36 years of Sarah's life. Over 160 rooms, in various states of completion, make up this rambling mansion. Doorways open to blank walls; stairways go up to the ceiling; secret passageways twist around to new wings; hidden windows in the floors allowed spying on the servants; and, adding to the mysterious atmosphere, there are 13s everywhere — 13-stepped stairways, 13 bathrooms, chandeliers with 13 lights, ceilings with 13 panels, rooms with 13 windows. The Tiffany crystal windows, gold and silver chandeliers, inlaid doors, parquet floors, attest to Sarah's good taste and bottomless pocketbook. The house tour takes an hour. A two-hour tour includes gardens, fountains, statues, water tower, pump house, greenhouse, and garage — a storeroom for the building supplies Sarah never got a chance to use.

The museum features handguns and rifles, antiques, and life size wax dioramas of the Winchester family and some of the people who used their hardware: Annie Oakley and Buffalo Bill, Butch Cassidy and the Sundance Kid, and Teddy Roosevelt.

Lick Observatory

Mount Hamilton, Hwy. 130, 25 miles Southeast of San Jose. Tel. 274-5061 (recording), 429-2513. Free tours daily, 1-5 P.M.

● A long narrow, winding road takes you to the top of Mount Hamilton and the awesome domes of Lick Observatory. It was here that the 5th moon of Jupiter was discovered — the first one since the time of Galileo. The visitor's gallery looks up at one of the largest telescopes (120 inches) in the world, and the tour of photos & the telescopes, astronomical instruments and 36-inch refractor is intriguing and educational. Star gazing is possible for the public on Friday nights in summer, but you must write (Visitors Program, Lick Observatory, Mt. Hamilton, CA 95140), with self-addressed, stamped envelope, for up to 6 tickets in advance.

New Almaden Museum

21570 Almaden Rd., New Almaden. Tel. 268-7869. Mon.-Fri., 1-4 P.M.; weekends and holidays, 10 A.M.-5 P.M. closed during school year Wed., Dec. & Jan. Adults, $1.25; under 16, 45¢.

● The New Almaden mine was the first mercury mine in California. The woman who owns the mine has gathered together mementos of the Indians and the Mexicans and American pioneers who lived in the area. She frequently gives interesting tour-talks through the museum, telling stories about the Indian dresses and artifacts, miners' tools and lunch pails, antique toys, sample ores and old Mexican objects that are exhibited. Be sure to see the barrel organ used by the padres to attract Indians.

Public Relations Tours

Pacific Press Publishing Association

1350 Villa St., Mountain View. Tel. 961-2323. Free tours (by appt.) weekdays.

● Learn how books are made and see editors, artists, compositors and binders at work.

Palo Alto Airport

1901 Embarcadero Rd., Palo Alto. Tel. 321-3330. Free tours (by appt.).

● You can even get into the control tower if you make an additional call and appointment at 327-7776.

Safe-T-Pacific

2500 Middlefield Rd., Redwood City. Tel. 369-6211. Free tours (by appt.) weekdays, 9:30-11:30 A.M. and 2-4 P.M.

● This 15-minute tour will tell you everything you want to know — maybe more — about the making of ice cream cones.

U.S. Weather Service

Bayshore Freeway, San Mateo. San Francisco International Airport, (P.O. Box 8247,) Tel. 876-2886. Free tours (by appt.) daily, any hour.

● See the materials used in briefing pilots and the weather teletypes and instruments.

6

THE SANTA CRUZ AREA

The Santa Cruz Area is small, nestled west of San Jose and north of Monterey. Big Basin Redwoods, Boulder Creek, and Loch Lomond are some of the natural sites of interest, and the village-cities of Watsonville and Castroville, home of the artichoke, are warm and welcoming. In Santa Cruz beaches are of major interest. Be sure to have some car games with you — the drive from San Francisco can be long and slow.

Santa Cruz City Museum

1305 East Cliff Drive, Santa Cruz. Tel. 423-7338. Daily, 10 A.M.-5 P.M., noon-5 P.M., winter. Free.

● Baskets and artifacts from the Eskimo and California Indians and reminders of the Mission days are just part of this excellent collection. There are special temporary exhibits, such as a touchable exhibit of acorn mash and grinding rocks and a microscope to use on feathers and shells. There are mammoth tusks and a mastadon tooth. The Glenn W. Brandt Junior Museum Wing houses live and stuffed mammals, including a Degus from Peru, the world's only small mammal with true color vision, birds, reptiles and insects. Turtle doves and golden eagles, genealogical trees of the animal kingdom, a buffalo and a sea lion and rare shellfish are children's favorites in this wing of an outstanding museum.

Santa Cruz Beach & Boardwalk

Riverside Ave. Beach St., Santa Cruz. Tel. 423-5590. Daily, 11 A.M.-11 P.M., summer; weekends, noon to 10 P.M., spring and fall; to 5 P.M., winter; weekends 12-5; closed Dec. Free.

● Last of the old-time boardwalks, Santa Cruz Playland has everything you would hope to find in one. You can ride a ferris wheel or a roller coaster, scoot around in little cars, make spin art, play skeet ball or miniature golf, watch marionettes, visit the penny arcade, and eat cotton candy, tacos, candied apples and corndogs on the run or lunch at sit-down restaurants. Or you could take a long quiet walk on the sandy beach. Crowds and prices change with the seasons. The merry-go-round is one of the nicest in California.

This sheltered beach is one of the finest public beaches in northern California. When the tide is out, you can walk among the tidepools along the foot of the cliff leading to the lighthouse.

The Santa Cruz Wharf is a great spot to fish and watch the seals playing and snoozing in the wharf pilings.

The Mystery Spot

1953 Branciforte Drive, Santa Cruz. Tel. 423-8897. Daily, 9 A.M.-6 P.M., summer; to 5, winter. Adults, $1.50; under 12, 75¢

● All the laws of gravity seem to be challenged in this strange natural curiosity. Even the trees do not stand up straight, and a visitor always seems to be standing backwards or sideways. One test here is to lay a carpenter's level across two cement blocks, seeing that their tops are on the same level, then standing on one and seeing your companion on the other has suddenly grown or shrunk. This place is a short "stopping off" spot. Our kids did get a big kick out of walking up the walls of the cabin that looks cockeyed but is scientifically straight.

Santa's Village

Hwy. 17, Scotts Valley. Tel. 438-2250. Daily, 11 A.M.-5 P.M., summer; weekends and holidays after Labor Day. Adults $1.75; ages 4-16, 75¢. Admission & all-rides ticket, $3.60.

● Tucked away in a redwood forest, Santa's Village is a delightful land of fairytale. Santa himself greets his little visitors before they touch the icy North Pole, ride the bobsled or the reindeer-pulled sleigh, or visit the Good Witch in her Gingerbread House. Rides on a giant Christmas tree, an Old MacDonald's tractor or a giant snowball are a few of the other features. Santa's Mill Wheel Fun House is fun, particularly when the White Rabbit is your guide. The fallow deer, the dollhouse, a burro barn and goat pen and an antique car barn provide amusement for every age and taste. Rides are not included in the price of admission.

Santa's Village

Lost World

Hwy. 17, Scotts Valley. Open year round, 9-6; Adults $1; children 50¢.

● Dinosaur Land sounds more interesting than it is. The tyrannosaurus Rex, diplodocus, allosaurus and pterodon are patently plastic and not the least bit impressive. On the other hand, the Mystery Forest has appeared in "Believe It or Not" and *Popular Science* and is quite interesting: 70 live trees have been carefully bent and twisted into strange geometric and pictorial shapes. The Double Spectacle Tree, Double Heart Tree, Living Telephone Booth, King's Throne and Nine-Toed Tree are unbelievable. Lost World is the kind of place that's fine if you are passing by, but not a place to aim for.

Roaring Camp & Big Trees Narrow Gauge Railroad

Graham Hill & Mt. Hermon Rds., Felton. Tel. 335-4484. Grounds open 10 A.M. to 6 P.M. Adults, $3.50; ages 3-15, $1.75; annual pass, $10. Trout fishing: 85¢ per catch. Daily, Mid-June-Mid-Sept. & weekends & holidays Spring & Fall, every hour on the hour, from 11 A.M. to 4 P.M.

● Curving through redwood forests and over rattling wooden bridges, the original 1880 steam engine pulls old-fashioned excursion cars up and down hills and around sky-high trees. You can stop over at Bear Mountain to hike and picnic before returning to Roaring Camp on a later train. Back at the Camp, the shortest covered bridge in the world (36 feet) and a duck pond interest younger folk, while the old General Store — offering potbellied stoves, cast-iron toys, stick candy and old railroad books and magazines — intrigues the rest. The whole family would enjoy Saturday and Sunday afternoons at Roaring Camp, when a chuckwagon barbecue from 11 to 4, May-Oct. is accompanied by the old-time country music (hamburgers, $2.95; steak, $4.95.) Picnic tables and group rates available.

William H. Volck Memorial Museum

Pajaro Valley Historical Association, 261 E. 3rd (Beach) St., Watsonville, Tel. 772-0305. Wed., Sat. and Sun. 2-4 P.M.

● This lovely old house, given to the Association by Mrs. Volck, is truly a community museum. One of the biggest treasures is a large 1887 photograph of two young girls, Rhoda Anne Rowe and Lorena Mabel Rowe. Historical sketches of Santa Cruz County, photos from the Watsonville school records, with biographies, commemorative pitchers, dishes and clothes used by pioneers, reticules, bisque dolls and glove boxes used by ladies in the town, cradleboards furniture and a photo of the first telephone office in Watsonville make up this very personal collection.

7

THE MONTEREY AREA

The Monterey area is many things — it's a surging arcadian seashore, a farm-rich industrial city, and a sweeping, windswept valley. Monterey is also the site of the first important Spanish settlement in California, and it was here that the state of California became part of the United States. Big Sur is probably the most magnificent seacoast in America. Salinas, the city most of us know from Steinbeck's *East of Eden* has more fascinating industrial tours than any other city we found in Northern California. And the valley that sweeps south from Salinas, to Soledad Mission, past Pinnacles National Monument, and on past San Antonio de Padua Mission, is just now developing into fertile farm land. A day, or a weekend, in this area could never do it justice.

San Juan Bautista SHP

San Juan Bautista State Historic Park

Tel. 623-4881. State Park: daily, 8:30 A.M.-5 P.M. Adult ticket, 25¢. Mission Museum: daily, 9:30 A.M.-5:30 P.M. $1 per family; adults, 50¢.

• A mission, a museum, an adobe house, an 1870s hotel and stables, a wash house, blacksmith shop, granary and wine-tasting room encircle the lovely plaza of San Juan Bautista. Start your visit at the mission, founded in 1797 and carefully preserved. The old adobe rooms house many treasures, including a 1737 barrel organ, gaming sticks of the San Juan Indians, the original kitchen and rawhide thongs and hand-shaped nails from the original building. The rose gardens and olive groves are peaceful retreats, as is the Indian burial ground behind the church. The church itself is bright and colorful, painted by a sailor who jumped ship and became the first U.S. citizen to settle in California.

Across the plaza is the Zanetta House, which once housed the Indian maidens of the settlement. The second floor was used as a public meeting room and dance hall. Visitors see fine china on the dining room table, a unique rocker in the living room and furnished bedrooms. Pass the wash house and adobe cottage to the nearby Plaza Stables where you can have fun rummaging through an assortment of carriages, wagons, harnesses, and mail pouches. The Stables also house General Castro's secretary's office. The Plaza Hotel next door is noted for its barroom, with billiard and poker tables at the ready. Wells Fargo memorabilia are displayed on the walls along with photographs and drawings of Indians, outlaws and Mexican and Yankee pioneers.

The Castro House should serve as a model for other museums; every room is completely labeled, with pictures to aid in the identification of its objects. The house is furnished as it was in the 1870s by the Breen family, who survived the Donner Party disaster to find a fortune in the gold fields. You'll see the candlesticks that came West with the Breens and the diary, wardrobe, wedding dress, gloves, fan, orange blossoms and card case of Isabella Breen. The kitchen is complete, down to the mouse trap on the floor and the laundry board in the sink.

The small town near the mission is full of old adobes and small interesting shops and restaurants, making San Juan Bautista a perfect place to spend a relaxing day.

San Luis Reservoir

Romero Overlook. Hwy. 152, between Hollister and Los Banos. Tel. 826-1196. Daily 9 A.M. to 7:30 P.M. Free.

• The history of this $600 million project is spread out before you, from the Indian artifacts found during the digging of the dam to the plant and viewing window of the generator. Movies and slide shows are presented, and a ranger will answer any questions you may have. Although the reservoir is rather out of the way, the scope of the project and its history make the extra time getting here worthwhile.

Monterey

● Fishermen's Wharf is a melange of restaurants, shops, fish stores and galleries. The crowds and store hours change with the season. Fishing and seal watching are favorite pastimes on the wharf. Sam's offers a 45-minute boat ride around the harbor for 75¢ for children and $1.50 for adults. There's also a diving bell for viewing the ocean floor.

● Cannery Row is a far cry from the Cannery Row John Steinbeck told us about. A growing complex of restaurants, shops and galleries fills the old buildings and offers entertainment for all. Step into *California Seasons* (379 Cannery Row, 372-5868) for free tastings of the original Monterey Jack cheese.

● If your children get tired of the historical sites and the seashore, they might enjoy a visit to the Dennis the Menace Playground (Lake El Estero, 372-8121, ext. 281, 10 A.M.-5 P.M. daily ex. Mon., free). There kids can swing on a suspension bridge, climb through a locomotive, grope through a maze and drink water from a lion's mouth.

Colton Hall

Dutra and King Sts., Monterey. Tel. 372-8121. Daily, 10 to 5. Free.

● Colton Hall, the first town hall and public school of Monterey, is famed as the site, in 1849, of the first constitutional congress of the new state of California. Here, the California Constitution was written in Spanish and English and the Great Seal of the state was designed and presented to the Congress. After that, Colton Hall became the County Seat of Monterey and, again, a public school. The large meeting room is furnished as it was at the signing of the Constitution. On the tables, there are biographies and portraits of each of the signers, which includes Ord, Sutter, Ellis, Larkin and Vallejo. A 26-star flag flies. In the anteroom are photos of the children who attended school here in the 1880s and the original drawing of the California bear by Charles Nahl.

Behind Colton Hall is the old *Monterey Jail*, open to the public daily until 4:30. The walls are thick stone, the doors iron and the cells pitch black and scary. It is impossible to believe that this was used as the city jail until May 1959, but that's what the sign says.

Allen Knight Maritime Museum

550 Calle Principal, Monterey. Tel. 375-2553. Tues.-Fri., 10 A.M.-noon & 2-4 P.M.; Sat. & Sun. 2-4 P.M. Free.

● A captain's cabin from an old sailing ship with bed, writing desk and sailor's ditty box, sets the proper mood for this three-room nautical museum. Models, photos, lithographs, paintings and various old sailing materials, octants, ships' bells, sailor's thimbles, Arctic goggles, scrimshaw and ship's logs are some of the items on display. One exhibit pictures all the ships that have visited Monterey harbor. There are sailing ships, steam ships, U.S. Navy and Air Force ships, fishermen and freighters. There's even a sardine boat in which to "pretend sail."

California's First Theater

Scott and Pacific Sts., Monterey. Tel. 373-2103. Box Office, Wed.-Sun., 1-8 P.M. call 375-4916. Daily, 9 A.M.-5 P.M., ex. Mon. Adult ticket, 25¢ usable at all state buildings that day.

● Jack Swan's lodging house gave its first performance of a stage play in 1847 to entertain bored soldiers. Since then, theatrical productions have been produced regularly and now 19th-century melodramas are performed on weekends. During the day, a ranger shows you through the theater, the backrooms and the main office/museum/barroom. He doesn't give a "guided tour lecture" — he talks with you about what you'd like to know, a much nicer way to do things. He'll tell you that they used to serve hot peanuts until the villain of the plays complained about being hit, that Lola Montez visited Monterey (and why). You'll learn where Swan got his 1800 hurdy-gurdy and all about the posters, bottles, song sheets and photos displayed on the walls. Several present-day movie heroes made their acting debuts here with the Troupers of the Gold Coast. If you look carefully, you can spot them on recent billboards.

Casa Del Oro

Corner of Scott and Olivier Sts., Monterey. Tel. 373-2103. Daily, 10 A.M.-5 P.M. Free.

● Thomas Larkin built this trading store in 1845; and, during the gold rush, when the big iron safe stored the miners' gold, the building became known as "the house of gold." Visitors can stand at the door to look at this fully equipped general store of the last century. Sewing machines and furniture are piled high, with chairs hanging from the rafters. Bags of coffee, bolts of cloth, cans of milk, and barrels of food wait for customers. Located between the First Theater and the Pacific Building, Casa Del Oro offers an interesting few minutes of history.

The Custom House

1 Custom House Plaza, 115 Alvarado St., Monterey. Tel. 373-2103. Daily, 10 A.M.-5 P.M. Free.

● The United States flag was first officially raised in California on this roof in 1846. Today, you walk into a long room that holds the exact duplicate of the cargo Richard Henry Dana wrote about in his *Two Years Before the Mast*. There are casks of liquor, cases of dishes, bags of nails, coffee and flour and wheels for wagons. A screeching yellow and green parrot lords over ribbons, ropes, cloth, soap, paper, tools and trunks. In one corner are piles of "California bank notes" — the cowhides used for trading. The Custom

Youth Science Center of Monterey County

House manager's quarters upstairs feature a comfortable carved bed and chest, a table and a desk with an open book and a cigar ready to be lit.

The Larkin House

Jefferson St. and Calle Principal, Monterey. Tel. 373-2103. Daily ex. Tues. 9:15 A.M.*-5* P.M.*, 35-minute guided tours only. Adults 25¢.*

● Small children are not really appreciated in this house. Built by Thomas Oliver Larkin, first and only U.S. consul to Mexico in Monterey, the house is an architectural and historical gem. It was the first home in Monterey to follow the New England style as well as the first to have glass windows. Many of the furnishings are original Larkin items.

Next door, through a rose-covered garden, is the small home used by William Tecumseh Sherman, a lieutenant in 1847-49. The house now serves as a waiting room for the Larkin House tour and as a small museum of Sherman's and Larkin's roles in California history. Here you learn that Sherman promised to return to lovely Dona Maria Ignacio Bonifacio. She planted a rose to bloom when he returned. And although the Sherman rose has bloomed yearly ever since, Sherman never returned. Dona Maria always remained true to his memory.

The Pacific Building

8 Custom House Plaza, Scott St. and Calle Principal, Monterey. Tel. 373-2103. Daily, 10 A.M.*-5* P.M. *Adult ticket, 25¢ usable at all state buildings that day.*

● The first floor of this supply house/ tavern/ court/ newspaper/ church/ ballroom is now a museum of California history. Photos, plaques and relic-filled cases are arranged chronologically, beginning with the Costanoan Indians. Spanish saddles and money, gold miners' and trappers' tools, the Victorian furniture of the American pioneers and the cargo and machinery of the whalers and loggers are all represented in this charming museum.

Upstairs is the Holman Collection, a remarkable gathering of Indian relics from all over North America. Mexican Indians and Alaskan Eskimo are included, but the local Costanoans rank first. Their religion, hunting, fishing, gathering and processing acorns, housing, trade, warfare, transportation and survival lessons are explained with artifacts and models. Visitors can compare the arrows, games, beads and baskets of many different tribes. The peoples of the Peninsula, past and present, are pictured with their pottery, picnics, parades and patriotism.

Information on this building, and all the state buildings in Monterey, may be found next door at 210 Oliver St.

Sancho Panza Restaurant

Casa Gutierrez, 590 Calle Principal. Monterey. Tel. 375-0095. Daily 11-2; 5-9; Sat. and Sun., 11-9.

● Built in 1841 by a young Mexican for his bride, this old adobe is now a comfortable Mexican country inn that looks like what an average citizen's home was like in Monterey. A warm fire blazes on cool evenings and there's a garden in back for lunch and for dinner on summer nights. Prices are reasonable and the food is very good. Large combination plates of Mexican specialties are $2 and up. Cool wine is poured from huge kegs near the door. Mexican/American newspapers are used as place mats and conversation pieces. At the end of the meal, top it off with Chocolato Mejicano — crushed almonds and cinnamon in frothy hot chocolate.

The Stevenson House

530 Houston St. Monterey. Tel. 373-2103. Tours every hour on the hour, daily, 10 A.M. to 4 P.M. Free.

● Robert Louis Stevenson spent a few months in a second-floor room of this boarding house during 1879. He had traveled from Scotland to visit Fanny Osbourne, who became his wife. He wrote *The Old Pacific Capital* in this room and the house, restored to look as it did then, is filled with Stevenson memorabilia. Upstairs, at the foot of the bed in the children's room, a ghostly spirit is sometimes spotted. Perhaps you'll be lucky enough to see her. The lovely garden makes a nice waiting room.

Pacific Grove Museum of Natural History

Forest and Central Aves., Pacific Grove. Tel. 372-4212. Daily ex. Mon., 10 A.M.-5 P.M. Free.

● Each October, thousands of Monarch butterflies arrive in Pacific Grove to winter in a grove of pine trees. Visitors who arrive in other months, or don't want to climb a pine tree, can see a marvelous exhibit on the Monarch in this museum. There is also a large collection of tropical and other California butterflies. Monterey sea otters, fish, shellfish, mammals, rodents, insects and birds are also displayed in stuffed models and photos. The skeleton of a sea otter is particularly touching. The geology of the county is well-illustrated with a relief map of Monterey Bay, fossils, ore and minerals, along with an introduction to crystallography.

Point Pinos Lighthouse

Off 17 Mile Drive, Pacific Grove. Tel. 372-3431. Sat., Sun., and holidays, 1-4 P.M. in summer. Free.

● The oldest lighthouse (1855) on the West Coast, Point Pinos overlooks the meadows and sand-dunes of a golf course on one side and the white-capped ocean on the other. A small U.S. Coast Guard maritime museum is open to the public upstairs, and downstairs a modern computer-operated signal is sent out to fog-bound ships.

Nearby, on the way into town, *Lovers Point* offers marine gardens, a small rocky beach, tree-shaded picnic grounds and glass-bottomed boats in summer.

U.S. Army Museum

The Presidio, Monterey. Tel. 242-8547. Thurs.-Mon., 9-12:30 & 1:30-4 P.M. Free.

● This Army-run museum displays the history of old Fort Hill from the Ohlone Indian period to the present. Monuments to Commander John Drake Sloat and Father Junipero Serra adjoin the museum. Ten history sites are located near the museum: Rumsen village sites and ceremonial rock; Fra Serra's landing place, and the ruins of the first American fort in Monterey. The museum collection includes uniforms from the turn of the century, swords, sabers and other army equipment, and dioramas of early forts and the first Presidio. The dioramas of Fort Costello and Fort Mervine are appropriate and interesting.

Carmel

● A visit to the Monterey Peninsula is not complete without an hour or two of browsing in the picturesque village of Carmel. The Pine Inn Block, bounded by Ocean Avenue, Lincoln Monte Verde and 6th Avenue, is an ever-changing scene of Victorian shops, gardens and restaurants. Of special interest to the children: *Sylvia's Danish Pastry Shop* (6th and Dolores, 624-1198) for creamy goodies; *The Carmel Butcher Shop* (Lincoln and Ocean, 624-2569) for rare hamburgers and garlicky spare ribs; *The Gallery of Fine Comic Art* (5th & Dolores) featuring original drawings of Dennis the Menace, Peanuts, Broom Hilda, et al; *Thinker Toys* (Carmel Plaza) for a den of educational and imported toys, puppets and the biggest collection of doll-house furnishings we've ever seen; *Seals and Owls* (Mission and Ocean, 625-1110) for arts and crafts of the Eskimos and American Indians; and *Swensen's Ice Cream Parlor* (Mission and Ocean, 624-8711); and be sure to visit The Magic Fishbone (Mission and 7th), known as the finest bookshop devoted exclusively to children in the country. After this tour, you shouldn't miss the Carmel beach at the end of Ocean Avenue. It is one of the most beautiful (non-swimmable) on the coast.

Thunderbird Book Shop & Restaurant

3½ miles out, Carmel Valley Road, Carmel. Tel. 624-1803. 9:30 A.M.-10 P.M. Tues.-Sat., until 5:30 P.M. Mon.; noon-5 P.M. Sun.

● The Thunderbird Book Shop is just what you dream a book store might be — a place where browsing is welcomed and the selection of books for children and adults is phenomenal. Upstairs is a unique collection of oriental antiques and Japanese folk art. One corner of the store is a restaurant, serving lunch and dinner Tuesday through Saturday. Dinner is salad with unusual dressings, popovers, roast beef, wild rice, relishes, coffee and sherbet. Lentil soup with a salad and a hot popover is $1 and you are invited to dally during your meal over a game of chess or checkers.

Mission San Carlos Borromeo

Rio Road off Hwy. 1, Carmel. Tel. 624-3600. Weekdays, 9:30 A.M.-5 P.M.; Sun. and holidays, 10:30 A.M.-5 P.M. Free.

Mission San Carlos Borromeo

● The lovely Mission church and cemetery, two museums and the adobe home of the pioneer Munras family combine to give this mission much of interest. Fra Junipero Serra rests in the church and in the cemetery lies Old Gabriel, 151 years old, baptized by Fra Serra. A small museum in the garden houses pictures of the original mission and its restoration. There are Indian grinding pots, arrowheads, baskets, beads, toys — and two Indian skeletons buried with eagle claws and turtles. The long main museum houses fine art from the original mission and a replica of the stark cell Fra Serra died in. You'll also find California's first library here — Serra's books, bibles, theologies, sermons, travel commentary, lives of saints and technical works. Altar pieces, saddles, the furnished kitchen and dining room of the padres and some of the mission priests' vestments are featured as well.

The *Casa Munras* is now a memorial to the Munras family. There are keys from the original adobe, embroidery, family pictures, music and provision boxes, jewelry, maps, chocolate pots and dresses. The Munras living room is furnished with a cradle and doll buggy, Victorian ornaments, a marble fireplace and handsome carved furniture.

Point Lobos State Reserve

Rt. 1, South of Carmel. Tel. 624-4909. Daily, opens 9 A.M. closes 4 P.M. Nov.-Mar.; 5 P.M. Apr. & Oct.; 6 P.M. May & June; 7 P.M. July-Aug. Guided tours twice daily in summer. $1 per car.

● The harsh barking of the sea lions offshore gives its name to this rocky and sea-ravaged point of land — "Punta de los Lobos Marinos," Point of the Sea Wolves. On lucky days, you can still hear the sea lions and see them frolicking on the rocks. Point Lobos is an outdoor museum; each tree, plant, and shrub is identified and protected by law, as are the cormorants, pelicans, gulls, squirrels, and black-tailed deer living here. The last natural grove of Monterey Cypress stands here. Picnicking and watersports are allowed in specified areas, and the several trails have detailed brochures to accompany you on a self-guided tour. During our walk, on a rainy April day, we saw four deer.

John Steinbeck House.

132 Central Ave., Salinas. Tel. 424-2735.

● John Steinbeck's childhood Victorian home is now a lunch restaurant with seatings at 11:45 or 1:15, Mon.-Fri. ($3+ dessert). Profits go toward the Valley Historical Guild restorations. Reservations are necessary.

Youth Science Center of Monterey County

544 River Rd., Salinas. Tel. 455-1776. Tues.-Fri., 9 A.M.-noon; Sat., 10 A.M.-2 P.M. Free.

● This junior museum and school specializes in the natural history of Monterey County. Over 100 of the region's birds and animals are on exhibit, including live toads, frogs, snakes and lizards. A "petting and snuggling" library, from which local kids can check out rabbits, hamsters, rats and guinea pigs, is always open to visitors. Lessons on ecology, biology and environment are available on a formal or informal basis. An Indian village with brush houses, a sweat lodge, a fire area and an acorn granary, is in the works, as are indoor and outdoor ponds with local fish and invertebrates.

Boronda Adobe

Boronda Rd. at W. Laurel Drive, Salinas.

● The Monterey County Historical Society is now restoring the home of Don Manuel de Boronda, a native of Spain who came to California as a corporal in the early 1800s. Letters, artifacts, photos, maps and documents of the Boronda Family will be displayed, along with old costumes, lettuce brands and silent movies of early lettuce farming, W.W.I "home movies," native American baskets, mortar & pestles of Stone Age Man found in Monterey County, old election posters, photos and records of the 1936 lettuce strike & riot, and old railroad tools.

Pinnacles National Monument

Off 101 at King City east. Tel. 389-4578. $1 per car per day.

● Entered from Soledad or King City, Pinnacles National Monument is a little-known land of striking beauty. Its 14,000 acres are comparable in rock formations and color striations only to the Grand Canyon. The fern glens, caves, wild animals and the curious pinnacles themselves, some 1,200 feet above the canyon floors, make this a perfect hiking spot (although in summer it's much too hot to be enjoyable). The map from the Visitors' Center shows short-looped trails as well as more strenuous trips up to High Peaks Trail.

Mission San Antonio de Padua

Jolon. (off Hwy. 101 from King City) Mon.-Sat.; 9:30 A.M.-4:30 P.M.; Sun 11 A.M.-5 P.M. Donation.

● In its "Valley of the Oaks," San Antonio de Padua is the most interesting mission in Northern California. It still functions as a working mission, with olive and vine presses, fields planted and stock roaming the hills, just as it has been since 1771. Inside the mission museum, you may read a Book of Baptism in Fra Junipero Serra's own hand, walk through the candle- and soap-making rooms, visit a sample mission bedroom and the kitchens, and climb up to the original wine vat. On the mission grounds, you will find beehive ovens, Temescal sweat houses, the aqueduct system & water wheel, and restored wine vat.

Public Relations Tours

Peter Paul Candy Factory

1800 So. Abbott, Salinas. Tel. 424-0481. 30 minute tours Tues. & Thurs., 10 A.M., and by appt. Free. For children over 8.

● It's hard to believe this beautifully designed building is a factory, but it's a candy manufactory, with the most tantalizing smells. Before the tour, white bakers' hats are passed out as souvenirs. The tour winds around vats of chocolate, sugar and corn syrup, under conveyor belts of coconut and rice crispies, past mixers and steam-jacketed kettles and into a room where almonds are shaken, dusted, roasted and chocolate-covered. Every day The Peter Paul Factory uses 26,000 pounds of chocolate. At the end of the tour, two full-size candy bars satisfy your inevitable craving for a sample.

Schilling Spices

1311 Schilling Place, Salinas. Tel. 738-2411. Tours Tues. & Thurs., 1 P.M., and by appt. (over 12 only). Free.

● Visitors see spices cleaned, processed, mixed, packaged, labeled, and boxed. Small samples (we got a mixture for salads) are presented at the end of the tour.

Forestiere Gardens

8

THE FRESNO AREA

There are those who say that Fresno exists as a stopping off place from San Francisco to Los Angeles. But it's a big, booming city, with lots of good Armenian restaurants and a beautiful city park. The trip to Fresno is a good long four hours from San Francisco, but there are so many motels in the city you can usually be assured of a room when you arrive. Surrounded by rich farmland, pretty lakes and an impressive irrigation system, Fresno is also the entrance to Sequoia National Park, Kings Canyon National Park, Sierra National Forest and Yosemite National Park.

R.C. Baker Memorial Museum

297 W. Elm St., Coalinga. Tel. 935-1914. Mon.-Fri., 9 A.M.-noon, 1-5 P.M.; Sat. 11 A.M.-5 P.M.; Sun. 1-5 P.M. Free.

• The R.C. Baker Museum, named in honor of a Coalinga pioneer, oil-man and inventor, shows both the natural and "man-made" history of Coalinga. The land surrounding Coalinga is rich with oil and minerals and the museum emphasizes these assets. The oil is also responsible for the numerous well-preserved fossils found near here, including mastodon skeletons and an oil-preserved primeval lizard. Artifacts of the first men to live here, the Tachi tribe of the Yokuk nation, include evidence that they used oil for trading. The crowded 1910 kitchen, 1880 advertising cards, and an old doll collection are fascinating. Two of the most unusual treasures are 600 kinds of barbed wire dating from 1867 and a 1908 quilt made of silk swatches that were packed in Nebo Cigarettes. There's even a "surrey with the fringe on top." The back room holds tools and machinery used in the oil fields. Visitors to Coalinga will enjoy a drive 9 miles north on Hwys. 33 & 198 past the Grasshopper oil pumps — oil field characters painted in many colors to look like clowns, birds, and animals.

Lindsay Olive Growers

620 N.Westwood, Lindsay. Tel. 562-5121. Mon.-Fri., every hour, 9-11 A.M. 1-4 P.M. Plant closed May-Aug.

● Do the kids like olives? Then they'll love this tasting, learning experience. In the hour walk through the plant, visitors learn the history of olive growing in California and the processing and packaging of this delicious fruit. The olives are washed down sloughs of California redwood into a barrel of brine for aging and then cooked for seven days in bubbling salt water until they're black and shiny. The tasting room offers relishes and pimento-filled, black and ripe green olives. When we were there, a class of fourth graders descended and finished every speck on the tasting table in three minutes.

Tulare County Museum

Mooney Grove Park, Tulare. Tel. 734-6151. Mon.-Fri. 9 A.M.-5 P.M., April 1-Oct. 15. Weekend all year 9 A.M.-6 P.M., 26¢.

● "End of the Trail," the bronze sculpture by James Earl Fraser portraying a tired Indian on a pony — once the most copied piece of art in the world — is the star attraction at this lively museum. The sculpture, and "Pioneer" were first exhibited in San Francisco in 1919 at the Pan-Pacific Exposition. A one-room school house, newspaper and dental office and rooms from turn-of-the-century homes recreate history. Furniture, clothes, cooking utensils, toys, baskets, W.W.I uniforms and early farm machinery are also exhibited. No wonder this museum won the 1974 Award of Merit from the California Historical Society.

Outside, the 143 acre park offers picnic arbors under oak trees, free boating on the lake, skateboard tracks, and more. (School groups are free.)

The Depot Restaurant

Railway Square, Visalia. 207 East Oak St. Tel. 732-8611. Lunch 11 A.M.-2:30 P.M.; Dinner 6-10 P.M.

● The old Visalia train station across the street from the museum is now a handsome restaurant with a railroad motif. The lunch menu, in the shape of an engine, offers "Pullman Pleaser" and "Brass-Pounder" burgers, as well as salads and sandwiches. The dinner menu is more versatile, with such main courses as the "Caboose Special" (prime rib) and "Engineer's Delight" (filet and lobster). For desert, the meringue-type grasshopper pie is superb. First courses are served on locomotive-stamped pewter plates.

Porterville Historical Museum

257 No. D St., Porterville. Tel. 784-9771. Thurs., Fri., and Sat., 10 A.M.-5 P.M. Free.

● The old Southern Pacific Railroad Station is now an interesting accumulation of historical artifacts of the Porterville pioneers. An original land grant certificate, an 1890 wedding dress, an 1870 corn-sheller, and old dolls are found in the main room. Old furniture, typewriters, early office machines and the first switchboard of the Porterville Hotel are in the back rooms. There are also Indian blankets, baskets and beadwork, along with stuffed animals indigenous to the county — a California condor, a golden eagle, mountain lions, bay lynx and birds. (By the way, we actually saw one of the rare condors on the road to Porterville.) The complete turn-of-the-century pharmacy makes you wonder how anyone managed to stay healthy. Fire wagons, covered wagons and farming, carpenter and mining tools are displayed on the grounds. A gracious lady, who knows all about Porterville's first families, enjoys telling the stories behind the treasures over which she presides.

Sun Maid Raisin Growers

13525 South Bethel Ave. off old Hwy. 99 Kingsburg. Tel. 897-5861. Tours by appt. Free.

● Children of all ages are made most welcome here. Hostesses in the Sun Maid costumes escort tours that end in the sample room. Visitors are also given samples to take home.

Forestiere Underground Gardens

5201 W. Shaw Ave. (at Freeway 99), Fresno. Tel. 485-3281. Tours every hour on the hour, June-Sept. 9:30-5 daily; Nov.-April 10-4 weekends & holidays, vacations Oct. & May Wed-Fri. 10, 12, 1 & 2; weather permitting; Adults, $2.50, ages 13-17, $1.25, ages 5-12, $1.

● Sicilian immigrant Baldasare Forestiere, a prosperous vineyardist and horticulturist, devoted his life to creating his own very individual lifestyle. When he decided that he couldn't bear the Fresno summer heat, he dug out a small underground room — and then kept digging until, 40 years later, he had a seven-acre underground estate. Visitors wind through an amazing network of rooms, courts, patios and passageways to view the strange and quite incredible fruit trees that Forestiere created in his underground gardens. One tree grows seven fruits — Valencia and navel oranges, grapefruits, sweet and sour lemons, cheedro, (a Sicilian rind fruit,) and tangerines. Fig trees grow roots from one room to another and many more varieties — dates, pomegranates, loquats, carob trees, oriental jujubes, flowering quince, Italian pears — bend to the skylights. You also see Forestiere's living quarters and furnishings and the ponds in which he kept fish fresh for his dinner. No one finishes the tour without admiration for a man who had a dream — and dedicated his life to achieving it.

Fresno Arts Center

3033 East Yale Ave. Fresno. Tel. 485-4810. Daily, 10 A.M.-4:30 P.M., Tues.-Thurs. 7:30-9:30 P.M. Free.

• The Fresno Arts Center seeks to keep the San Joaquin Valley in tune with the intellectual and spiritual growth of the 20th century. Art from earlier centuries is occasionally shown, but the emphasis is on artists and craftsmen, both local and well-known, who are creating today. The children were especially intrigued with the yarn and leather wall hangings and, of course, they also enjoyed the display of children's art.

Fresno Museum of Natural History

1944 N. Winery Ave., Fresno. Tel. 251-5531. Tues.-Sat., 9 A.M.-5 P.M.; Sun. 12-5 P.M. Adults 50¢; ages 6-17, 25¢. Astronomy program, June-Aug. Free.

• This small museum has an extensive collection of native birds, mammals and reptiles, paleontological remains (dinosaur bones, fossils, sharks' teeth, sea lion skeletons) and Indian artifacts. The Indian room displays a real 100-year-old Yokut hut with toys, food, baskets and many other objects common to the household. An interesting large exhibit features the many things that the Indian has introduced to civilization, such as tobacco, lacrosse, snowshoes, dyes and foodstuffs like cranberries, pumpkins, tomatoes, turkey and cashews. The evolution of tools from the prehistoric Indians to the present is also fascinating. Dioramas of lake and valley birds and animals in their natural surroundings are accompanied by questions to learn by and the geology of Fresno and the San Joaquin Valley and the forming of storms in the skies are explored in clever and educational exhibits.

Bar 20 Dairy Farm

4260 West Madison Ave., Fresno. Tel. 264-0472. Daily, 12-5 P.M. Tours by appt. Free.

• On your way to the Kearney home, stop off for a moment to see how cows are milked. The Bar 20 is a quiet working farm, with one long gray building at the end of the driveway that is open to the public for "cow-viewing." One wall of the building is glass so that you can see the cows as they line up to be washed, milked by machine, fed and corralled — on an assembly-line process. A taped explanation tells you what is happening — although it's all fairly obvious. In the corral outside, you can watch the calves at play while the cows eat their dinner. This place used to be called Hopalong Cassidy's Bar 20 Ranch, but youngsters didn't know who Hopalong Cassidy was — so they dropped his name!

M. Theo Kearney Mansion

7160 W. Kearney Blvd. Kearney Park, Fresno. Tel. 264-8317 or 237-6755. Wed.-Sun., 2-4:30 P.M. Adults, $1; ages 6-18, 25¢. March-December.

● M. Theodore Kearney, the first president of the California Raisin Growers Association, was a late 19th-century industrialist who lived and spent well. A guide takes you past hand-blown Tiffany lamps, photos of Mr. Kearney with his luxurious cars and his old flame, Lillie Langtry, and his office safe with floors of concrete 5 feet thick. A Mother Goose book, 1908 dictionary, feather bed and shelf of toys are in the nursery. Listen to the piano roll in the dining room and note the buzzer on the arm of Kearney's chair, used to page the servants. The fully furnished bedrooms, with clothes laid out, make a visitor feel like the Kearneys have just stepped out and will be back any moment. The mansion is set in a lovely park with a tea house, playgrounds and picnic areas. There are special group tours for children (call 264-8317 for information).

Roeding Park

890 W. Belmont, Fresno. Tel. 488-1549. Roeding Park Zoo. Daily, 10 A.M.-5 P.M. Wed.-Sun. Over 14, 50¢.

● More than 550 birds, mammals and reptiles live in this neat little zoo. The aviary is green and open, with a walkway that allows you to see the birds "head-on." The door to the giraffes' shelter is marked with a scale of feet and inches so you can measure the giraffes as they come out, and the seals use a slide to swoop down into their pond. There are rare white rhinos, two pairs of orangutans with a baby, and a scimitar-horned oryx. You can peek in the nursery through a big glass window.

Storyland

Roeding Park, Tel. 264-2235. Daily, 10 A.M.-5 P.M., May-Oct., weekends in winter. Closed Dec. & Jan. 3 yrs. & up 50¢.

● Talking storybook keys (50¢) persuade the blue caterpillar to tell eight classic fairytales; and when the children have heard the stories, they can go on to visit the heroes of some of the tales. They can play in King Arthur's castle, Red Riding Hood's grandmother's cottage or Mr. Toad's cart; or they can talk to Simple Simon's pie man, the knights and knaves of Alice's court, the Three Bears or Little Miss Muffet. In this children's library come to life, little ones will walk the Crooked Mile, slide down Jack's

Beanstalk, climb the Owl's Tree, have a drink at Mother Goose's fountain and visit the lambs and rabbits in Mr. McGregor's Cabbage Patch.

Fort Millerton

Roeding Park, Fresno. Sat. & Sun., 2-5 P.M. Donation.

• This old blockhouse is, today, an exhibit on pioneer life. Visitors may see antique children's toys, the history of the lumber industry and the complete medical kit of Fresno's first doctor.

San Joaquin Fish Hatchery

Off Hwy. 41 east of Fresno. Tel. 822-2374. Daily, 8 A.M.-4 P.M. Free.

• There are more fish in this one spot than you'll ever see again. More than 2,000,000 trout, in sizes from pinhead to fingerling to almost catchable, are raised in these trout-hatching ponds. Four times a day the fish are fed a high-protein dry pellet; and when they're grown to 10 inches, after a year, they're taken in tanks by plane and truck to the heavily fished streams and lakes of California. But while they're here, it's really fun to walk along the 48 ponds and watch the fish leap over and slide down the little dams between them. A photo exhibit and recorded lecture explains trout habits and the trout-seeding program.

Friant Dam & Millerton Lake State Recreational Area

Off Hwy. 41 east of Fresno. Tel. 822-2212. Daily, dawn to dusk. $1 per car.

• Fed by Sierra snows, the waters of Millerton Lake are released into the Friant-Kern irrigation canals to feed the rich croplands of Fresno County. The dam is 319 feet high and 3,488 feet long, with a reservoir capacity of 5,200,000 gallons. You can walk half way across the dam and guides tell you the history of the dam project. Millerton Lake State Recreation Area offers boating, swimming, fishing, camping and picnic space, and the old *Millerton Courthouse*, overlooking Friant Dam, is a pleasant little museum of Friant history (open 1-5 P.M. on weekends, 25¢).

Yosemite Mt.-Sugar Pine Railroad

Hwy. 41, Yosemite Mt., Fish Camp. Tel. 683-7273. Daily, 10 A.M.-4 P.M., summer; weekends and holidays, weather permitting, 11 A.M.-4 P.M., Sept.-May. Adults, $2.50; ages 5-15, $1.25.

• Just 4 miles from Yosemite, this scenic, historic narrow-gauge steam railroad and logging train operates whenever weather permits. "The Logger," a Shay steam engine, wends its way through 4 miles of forest, past Slab Town Loop and Honey Hill and down to the bottom of a canyon. Visitors may stop off for a picnic or hike and return on a later

Friant Dam

train. A railroad museum and gift shop (conductor's hats, 10¢) are open in good weather. In winter, you can slide down hills on an inner tube and in summer, there are moonlight rides every Saturday night.

Yosemite National Park

(The Hwy. 120 entrance from Lee Vining on Interstate 395 through Tioga Pass is closed during the winter, which may last until May.)

Tel. 372-4461. Visitors Center: daily, 8 A.M.-10 P.M. Museums open daily in summer only. Cars: $3 a day.

• If you and your family had only one sight to see in California, your best choice would be Yosemite National Park. Yosemite is one of the world's wonders. The park seems to be a world within itself both for man and nature. Elevations range from less than 2,000 to over 13,000 feet and, in these 11,000 feet, five different plant belts exist. Each sustains a part of the park's wildlife population of 220 bird and 75 mammal species. In this natural splendor you can hike, swim, camp, fish, ski, ride horseback, bicycle or simply sightsee by car. Your first stop should be the Visitors Center in Yosemite Valley, where you can learn about the park from the center's pamphlets, exhibits, audio-visual programs, lectures and guided walks. Check *Yosemite Guide*, free, at entrance stations for latest schedule. One program with fireside stories and toasted marshmallows, was created especially for youngsters.

Where you go in Yosemite will, of course, depend on your time, interests and the time of year. You can choose from mountains, giant sequoia groves, towering waterfalls like Bridal Veil, and breathtaking vistas of Sentinel Rock and El Capitan. There are also museums in Yosemite for rainy days or for a change of pace. At the *Pioneer Yosemite History Center* at Wawona you can wander through a collection of horse-drawn vehicles, an old jail, a miner's hut, a working wagon shop and a covered bridge. The *Yosemite Travel Museum*, in the Administrative area near Arch Rock entrance, tells the story of early-day railroad and auto transportation in the Yosemite region. The Geology Museum (open daily in summer), at the Visitors Center in Yosemite Valley, shows how the mountains, waterfalls and gorges in Yosemite were formed. The natural history of Yosemite is also examined at the *Happy Isles Trail Center*.

Yosemite is always very crowded in July and August, so it is wise to plan your visit during June or September if you can. For information about the park, write to Superintendent, Yosemite National Park, Cal. (95389); tel. (209) 372-4461. Reservations are advised throughout the year at the park's hotels,

lodges, cabins and campsites. For details, contact Yosemite Park and Curry Company, Yosemite National Park, Cal. (95389), tel. (209) 372-4671. The Yosemite Natural History Association puts out a newspaper describing special events and giving a rundown of daily activities (subscription, $5). For road and weather information, call (209) 372-4222.

Bodie Ghost Town

State Historic Park, Bodie. Hwy. 395 south of Bridgeport (near Nevada border). Free.

• Nestled high in sagebrush country, Bodie has escaped all the commercialism found in most ghost towns of the West — it doesn't even have telephones. Information comes from a self-guiding tour pamphlet stowed in a container on the side of a building. The 170 original buildings that still stand are maintained in a state of arrested disintegration — neither restored nor allowed to decay further. You walk by the 1878 Methodist church, the windowless jail, the frame schoolhouse, a small house that belonged to President Hoover's brother and the iron vault of the bank, which was the scene of many exciting Old West hold-ups. Just wander through this quiet ramshackle town and imagine all the high adventures that occurred here more than a century ago. Be warned that Bodie is buried in snow in winter (we tried to get there in late April, but the roads were still closed).

Bodie Ghost Town SHP

9

THE STOCKTON AREA

The Stockton Area, below Sacramento, is the entrance to the Gold Country. Visitors will find rolling hills and good green farmland dotted by pleasant cities and villages. Stockton is named in honor of Commodore Robert Stockton, who led the forces which took over California for the United States in 1847. The little lakes and the peacefulness of the San Joaquin Valley add to the ambience of the area.

Mariposa County Historical Museum

Library Building, Hwy. 140 at 10th St. Mariposa. Tel. 966-2924. Daily ex. Sun., 10 A.M.-4 P.M.

● An Indian teepee in the front yard guides you to this gem of a museum. Inside, you'll find a newspaper office, assay office, saloon, drug store, and 1850's schoolroom — all furnished as they were in Gold Rush days. Toys, dolls, clothing, historical documents, and other artifacts of the local Indians are also on display. The people in charge of the museum enjoy talking about the people who had a part in developing Mariposa.

Mariposa County Courthouse

Mariposa. Tel. 966-2005. Tours weekends and holidays, 9:30 A.M.-4 P.M. Free.

• The clock in the tower of the county courthouse has been measuring the time since 1866. The building itself is the oldest courthouse still in use in California. Visitors walk through the courtroom — furnished today as it was 100 years ago — view the lovely old law library, and study a collection of Mariposa County gemstones and minerals.

Hershey Foods

1400 Albers Rd., Oakdale. Tel. 847-0381. Mon.-Fri., 8:15 A.M.-3 P.M. Free.

• Candy bars, chocolate kisses, and chocolate syrups are made, weighed, packaged, and labeled in the course of this 30-minute tour. You pass huge chocolate vats, candy-bar molds in action, and rooms for the processing of instant cocoa and chocolate syrup. Free candy bar to each visitor.

Miller Horse & Buggy Ranch

Hwy. 132, 9425 Yosemite Blvd. Modesto. Tel. 522-1781. Open whenever Mrs. Mae Miller is there, "which is most of the time." Adults 50¢; under 12, 25¢.

• This wagon collection and the 1900 general store are absolutely fascinating, but they are so cluttered and cobwebbed that some people may shy away. Those who climb in and poke around will be well-rewarded. Over 50 cars and wagons, including a fire-house grouping, are in the barn. There are stage coaches, beer wagons, an am-

bulance used in the San Francisco earthquake, racing sulkies, Victoria coaches, excursion buses and a "tally-ho" coach used in San Mateo for royalty. The 1906 "success" auto (with a place to hitch the horse, in case) and the Sears Roebuck order-by-catalog car are alone worth the price of admission. In the general store a hurdy-gurdy and high-button shoes, penny candy and coffee grinders, sausage stuffers and old magazines are piled high. The store also houses a typewriter collection and an amazing bicycle collection dating to 1820, including 3-, 4-, and 6-seaters and a mother-of-pearl tandem reputedly given to Lillian Russell by "Diamond Jim" Brady. There's also a barber shop and a blacksmith shop with everything in it but the smithy.

Pixie Woods

Louis Park, Stockton. Tel. 944-8220 / 466-9890. Weds.-Fri. and holidays, 11 A.M.-6 P.M., Sat. & Sun. noon-7 P.M., summer; Wed.-Sun. noon-5 P.M., spring; weekends and holidays, noon-5 P.M., fall; closed Nov. 24-Feb. 24. Adults, 25¢; under 12, 15¢. Boat ride, 20¢ train and merry-go-round 15¢.

• When you enter the rainbow gate of Pixie Woods, you enter a children's fairyland built entirely by the people of Stockton. Children can play in the castle, on the pirate ship, around the rocket ship, and on a fire engine. They can ride on a Chinese dragon, slide down a Princess tower, and talk to Little Miss Muffet. The Toad Stool theater gives free shows at 1:30, 3, and 4:30 P.M. and the volcano erupts every 15 minutes. At MacGregor's farm, there are chickens, turkeys, calves, rabbits, pigs, and sheep to pet and hold. An afternoon amid the flowers, brooks and bridges of Pixie Woods would be a total delight for small fry.

Pioneer Museum and Haggin Galleries

1201 No.Pershing Ave., Victory Park, Stockton. Tel. 462-4116. Daily ex. Mon., 1:30-5 P.M. Free.

• Three floors of history and art fill this handsome red brick building in Victory Park. Interpretive displays of California and local history include storefronts, vehicle galleries and an Indian Room. Indian artifacts, and a gun collection. Fossils and geological displays are here as well, and Stockton's history is seen through photographs and other memorabilia donated by local citizens. The gallery of American and European paintings and sculpture includes works by Albert Bierstadt, graphics & decorative arts. Victory Park offers a play area, duck pond, totem pole, and picnic tables.

Pollardville Ghost Town

10464 Hwy. 99, three miles above Stockton. Tel. 931-0272/931-4571. Weekends, noon to 6 P.M. Free.

• Pollardville Ghost Town is made up of both movie set and actual buildings brought down from the Mother Lode country. The Jamestown Jail was brought from Calavaras County and the Freedom Gazette newspaper building from Jackson. The Pollardville Hotel starred in the Gregory Peck movie *Big Country*. "Gunfights" are staged in the saloon and on the street and the Rock & Roll Railroad (40¢) barrels around town regularly. Visitors can see an 1880s livery stable, a dentist's and a doctor's office and an undertaker's establishment. The largest kerosene lamp collection in the world is inside the hotel. Vaudeville ("Love Rides the Rails") and melodrama are presented every Friday and Saturday night at the old Palace Theatre. The Chicken Kitchen, at the entrance, dispenses chicken dinners in an Old West atmosphere.

Micke Grove Park & Zoo

11793 No. Micke Grove Rd., 3 miles south of Lodi on Hwy. 50. Tel. 368-4641; museum, 368-9154. Zoo: 10 A.M.-5 P.M. daily. Park: dawn to dusk daily. 50¢ per car on weekends & holidays.

• The animals in the zoo are fed at 11, 1 and 3 every day for the amusement of the visitors — and the animals. Lions, bobcats, and bears of all sizes seem much too close for comfort in this nice little zoo. A swimming pool, an amusement park with lots of fun kiddie rides and peaceful rose and Japanese gardens add to the attraction of this pleasant park. The historical museum (368-9154) and picnic areas make you feel that you could spend a whole day here. The museum, with its memorabilia of pioneer families, including furniture, dolls and tools, is a good place to spend a rainy afternoon.

10

THE SACRAMENTO AREA

The Sacramento Area is the political heartland of the state of California. Two hours away from San Francisco, the city of Sacramento is worth a visit to see how the state functions — from the legislative rooms and state displays in the Capitol to the judicial buildings in Capitol Square. The state capital of California has been in Benicia, Vallejo and San Jose. Now, with the 100th anniversary of the Capitol building coming up in 1979, and the building of a new governor's mansion, Sacramento seems to be the permanent capital of the state. The green farmland surrounding the city is reflected in the 40-acre Capitol Park within the city, and visitors will appreciate the combination of rural and urban surroundings.

California State Capitol

Capitol Mall, Sacramento. Tel. 445-6070. Free tours of the East Wing Mon.-Fri. at 10:30 A.M. & 1:30 P.M.

● Visitors may look in on the Assembly and the Senate when the legislature is in session. Fifty-eight displays for each county in the state are on the ground floor of the East

Wing. The governor's office is right on the main floor, so you may spot him or some other celebrities.

E.B. Crocker Art Gallery

216 O Street, Sacramento. Tel. 446-4677. Daily, ex. Mon., 10 A.M.-5 P.M.; Tues. 2 to 10 P.M. Free.

● The oldest art gallery in the West was built in 1873 to house the paintings, and prints collected by Judge Edwin Bryant Crocker. The collection has grown since then and now includes prints from the Renaissance to the 19th century, pottery from the 5th century B.C. to the present, tapestries, crafts and sculpture. Aside from the permanent exhibits, there are several galleries devoted to changing exhibits of today's artists. Tile and parquet floors, rococo mirrors, frescoed ceilings, handcrafted woodwork and curving staircases make the building itself a work of art. Concerts, lectures and other special events are scheduled throughout the year.

Food Circus

1735 Arden Way, Arden Fair Shopping Center, Sacramento. Tel. 927-5092. Open for breakfast, lunch and dinner.

● You want a pizza, your spouse yearns for chow mein and the children want hamburgers? You can eat together at Food Circus — eight restaurants together under one roof. Here you can choose from Mexican, Chinese, German, Italian and American standbys of steak, fish and hamburgers, usually for under $3.

Fairytale Town

William Land Park, Sacramento. Tel. 449-5233. Tues.-Fri., 10 A.M.-6 P.M., weekends to 7 P.M., summer; daily ex. Mon., 10 A.M.-6 P.M., winter. Adults, 25¢; children, 15¢.

● Nursery rhymes and favorite stories all seem quite plausible in this small, cheerful land of make-believe. Youngsters can crawl through the holes of The Cheese or down the Rabbit's Hole, pet the baby goats at Troll Bridge, see Hiawatha, the Three Little Pigs, the Tortoise and the Hare and Mary's Little Lamb. The Japanese Garden, which represents a Japanese children's story, and the Children's Theatre, for puppet shows and skits, complete the array. Warnings from Fairytale Town: "Snails and turtles must be kept on a leash" and "You must not sit on the elves."

William Land Park Zoo

3930 West Land Park Drive, William Land Park, Sacramento. Tel. 447-5094. Daily, 9 A.M.-5 P.M. in winter, 9 A.M.-6 P.M. in summer. Adults 35¢; ages 13-17 25¢; ages 6-12, 15¢

● Almost 1,000 animals live in this tree-shaded garden and zoo. The reptile house, a curve of concrete, is a favorite; others are the wallaroos, 15 species of cats, the ring-tailed lemurs, and the island of monkeys. The river otters have a slide for speedy entry into their pond and the penguins swim smugly in an icy-cold pond.

Old Sacramento

● From I Street to L Street and from Interstate 5 to the Sacramento River, over 3 square blocks in this old area of town are being restored to their splendor at the time of the Gold Rush. Fanny Ann's Saloon, crammed with funky pictures, toys and knick-knacks is a popular hamburger spot. The new City and County Museum will trace the development of the area from pre-Spanish days to the present. A railroad museum, displaying equipment, photographs and actual rolling stock dating to the 1860s, is under construction at I and 2nd Streets, using hardware and bricks from the original building that stood there. Lucius Beebe's private car, Governor Stanford's private Engine #1 and the Gold Coast are three of the cars that will be on view. The old Morse Building now serves as the Gold Rush Theatre and the Huntington & Hopkins mercantile store will be reconstructed. Restaurants, galleries and shops make this a nice place to spend an afternoon.

Pioneer Hall — Sacramento City & County Museum

1009 7th St., Sacramento. Tel. 447-2908. Mon.-Fri. 9 A.M.-5 P.M. Sat. & Sun. 10 A.M.-4 P.M. Free.

● This 1860 Greek Revival building houses the history of Sacramento in photographs, lithographs and small relics from the Gold Rush to the present. The 1891 California State Fair, the development of agriculture and the growth of the education and culture of the state are depicted in interesting exhibits. Old toys, trading cards, clothing and an early crank washing machine are some of other items on display. The favorite of the boys was the iron-soled shoes worn by miners in the gold fields. This exhibit is scheduled to be moved to the reconstructed Old Sacramento soon.

Governor's Mansion

16th and H Streets, Sacramento. Tel. 445-4209. 10 A.M. to 4:30 P.M., by tour only. Over 18, 50¢.

● The official residence of California's governors from 1903 to 1967 is now a handsome Victorian museum. The half-hour guided tour is both a history of California and a look at the splendid old house. Living rooms, bedrooms, dining rooms and hallways are furnished in a melange of styles, reflecting the varying tastes of the thirteen governors who lived there. The old carriage house has also been converted to a museum (free) where you may see the hats, fans, parasols and other personal belongings of the governors and their families. Photographs and biographies of the governors line one wall. The garden is also a pleasant place to wait for your tour.

The Governor's Mansion

Sacramento Junior Museum

4500 Y St., Sacramento. Tel. 456-6417. Mon.-Sat., 9:30 A.M.-5 P.M.; Sun., 12 A.M.-5 P.M. Animal playtime: Sat. & Sun. 1:30 P.M. Planetarium show: Sat., 2 and 3, P.M. Sun. 2 P.M. Adults, 25¢; ages 3-15, 10¢.

● This junior museum is surprisingly small and disorganized for such a large community. Constantly changing programs include the art of basketweaving, learning canoe handling, nature photography, and wool fabric from fleece. The Animal Room also houses a jack rabbit, kangaroo rats, squirrels, chickens, kit and gray foxes, a coyote, guinea pigs, raccoons and Sam, the talking mynah bird.

State Indian Museum

2618 K St., Sacramento. Tel. 445-4209. Daily, 10 A.M.-5 P.M. Adult ticket, 25¢, usable at all state parks the same day.

● Next door to Sutter's Fort, this unassuming building houses what must be the best collection of California Indian relics in the state. The exhibits span archaeology, basketry, featherwork, pottery, maps, minerals, musical instruments, clothing, ceremonies, boats, housing and jewelry. Did you know that there were over 750 languages spoken by the Indians of North America? Do you know the tribes of Northern California? Here you'll see Maidus grinding acorns, a Mono storage shelter, a Pomo tule boat, a Miwok headdress and the ghost dance of the Sioux and Cheyenne. Ishi, last of his California tribe, is here in photographs, starting a fire, skinning a deer and painting, carving and sewing. Other civilizations were here before we were. This place makes you aware of how little we know of them.

Sutter's Fort

State Historic Park, 2701 L St., Sacramento. Tel. 645-4209. Daily, 10 A.M.-5 P.M. Adults, 50¢ (including info. wand); under 18, free (25¢ for info. wands).

● Sutter's Fort is one of the best places to relive California history. The fort and its buildings and stables are perfectly reconstructed and the cooperage, distillery, saddle shop, candlemaking room, kitchens, trading post, Indian guard room, vaqueros' bunk room, and Sutter's bachelor and family quarters are all exactly as they once were. The songs and information provided through the headsets are clear, helpful and entertaining. While facing a model of James Marshall showing Sutter the gold he found at the mill, you hear their conversation and Sutter's Swiss accent. A pioneer lady talks to herself as she bends over the stove, Indians sing while working at shuttle and loom. Live donkeys still stand in the stables and the fire still glows in the blacksmith shop. A small museum relates Sutter's biography and the life of the California pioneers. Our kids were especially taken with the diorama of John Fremont and Kit Carson entering the fort in 1844.

Folsom City Community Park & Zoo

50 Natoma St., Folsom. Tel. 985-3661, ext. 58. Daily, 10 A.M. to sundown. 35¢. A ⅓-scale live steam engine runs.

● Golden eagles, turkey vultures, great horned owls and hawks and pigeons fly free in large cages in this nice little zoo. Monkeys, coyotes, mountain lions, black bears, lions, tigers and ocelots prance in concrete cages. Deer and ponies graze in a nearby meadow. Pleasant picnic spots, a baseball field and a perky little train are added attractions in this community park.

Historic Sutter Street

Folsom.

● Old Folsom lives again in this restored section of old buildings and shops. The miniatures at Dorothea's Peppermint Lane, and Patsy's Soda Parlor take visitors back to gayer times, and the Sutter Gaslight Theater, a cider shop and Chinese, French and Italian restaurants make a short stay worthwhile. Nearby, at Sutter & Wool, is the reconstructed Southern Pacific depot with a display of historical memorabilia.

Public Relations Tours

California Almond Growers

18th and C. Streets, Sacramento. Tel. 442-6771. Tours Mon.-Fri., 10 A.M. and 2 P.M., Sat. and Sun., movie only at 11 A.M. & 3 P.M. Free.

● Franciscan fathers brought the almond with them to California in 1769. Today, Blue Diamond is the world's largest almond packer. The tour of the plant and a movie takes about one hour. Visitors see many unusual machines designed to sort, crack, halve, slice and dice roasted almonds. You see concrete bins eight stories high and a mile-long conveyor belt. Dig into at least ten different flavored almonds in the tasting room. (open 8 A.M.-5:30 P.M. daily). Our favorites are garlic/onion and honey/cinnamon.

Gibson Ranch County Park

8552 Gibson Ranch Rd., Elverta. Tel. 991-5322. Daily, 7 A.M. to dusk. Free.

● This 245-acre county park is really a working farm. There are cows, hens and horses. Muskrats, ducks, mudhens and geese swim in the 8-acre lake, which you can fish. There are ponies and donkeys and horses to ride (25¢ summer weekends), paddleboats to rent, and picnics and hayrides to enjoy. Tours by appt.

Folsom Project Dam and Powerplant

7806 Folsom-Auburn Rd., Folsom. Tel. 988-1707. June-Aug. 9 A.M.-4 P.M. Daily. Weekends May & Sept. By appt. Free.

● Drive on top of the dam, past the gorgeous lake, to get to the powerhouse. Tours past 3 generators with capacities of 66,240 kilowatts, each, and through the dam depending on how many people are visiting at the time. For tour appt. write Folsom Office, CVP, P.O. Box 37, Folsom, CA 95630.

In town on Riley St. is the historic Folsom Powerhouse that relayed electricity to Sacramento until 1952. (Call 988-0205 for appt.)

11

THE GOLD COUNTRY

———————

To drive along Highway 49 is to experience California's colorful history and legends. This is the Gold Country — the land of writers like Mark Twain and Joaquin Miller, bandits like Black Bart and Joaquin Murietta and heroes like Ulysses S. Grant and Horatio Alger. Passing through little towns named Copperopolis and Jenny Lind, visitors who look carefully will see the remembrances of the hundreds of thousands of people — Cornish, Welsh, English, German, French, Italian, Mexican, Peruvian, Australian, Chinese and African — who migrated here, seeking fame and fortune. The many parks and camping grounds are inevitably near quiet streams that were once gorged with gold panners. The town of Volcano still has an old Chinese store and a Jewish cemetery. The best thing to do in the Gold Country is just explore and perhaps talk to the natives; you'll have good experiences that you couldn't possibly find listed in a book and you'll hear about towns that now exist only in memory.

Coulterville Trading Post & Museum

Highway 49, Coulterville. Tel. 878-3438.

• Jars of hard candy, cold sarsaparilla, old guns, gold nuggets, and minerals, miners' provisions, and gold pans are sold at the Trading Post in Coulterville. Outside, the old Mary Harrison gold-mine locomotive rests near a cook's wagon and an old quartz gold mill. The Wells Fargo Building next door houses a unique collection of gold nuggets, quartz gold, pocket gold, octahedron gold crystals, and gold in volcanic mud. There's also a collection of minerals and crystals from the Mother Lode country. Here, the museum itself is arranged just like a 49er trading post, right down to the old trunks and the Wells Fargo bullion box stacked and ready for the next stage.

Railtown 1887 & The Sierra Railroad Co.

Railtown 1887, Jamestown. Tel. 984-5388. Railtown is open daily, 9 A.M.-5 P.M. summer; weekends, Apr. & Oct. Prices vary with each special train ride. Roundhouse tours.

• Every Saturday, May 1 to September 30, the Sierra's Mother Lode Cannonball steam engine speeds for an hour through the Mother Lode to the town of Chinese Camp or into tall pine woods to Fassler. Supper rides, charters and wine and cheese outings are also in the works. For tickets and information: Sierra RR, 781 South Washington St., Sonora (95370). For Information on the Sierra supper chief, call 983-2157 in San Francisco. The roundhouse and depot in the 27-acre museum of railroad shops have appeared in over 50 movies, so you may recognize them. A section of air-conditioned railroad dining cars and lounge cars serve refreshments.

Columbia State Historic Park

Hwy. 49, 4 miles north of Sonora, Columbia. Tel. 532-4301. Daily, 9 A.M.-5 P.M. Free.

• Columbia, "The Gem of the Southern Mines," is a restored goldmining town of the 1850s. The streets and wooden sidewalks lead you to buildings, stores and eateries outfitted as they were in the town's heyday. The Columbia Gazette office, open to the public on weekends and all summer, still prints a small newspaper; the Columbia Candy Kitchen still sells penny candy; and the 1857 Douglas Saloon still dispenses an occasional draft. Peek into the carpentry, the ice depot and the schoolhouse — furnished with bell tower, pump organ, desks and potbellied stoves. The Chinese herb shop, the fandango hall and the town jail and drugstore are all main street attractions. The Masonic Hall has pushbutton lectures that tell of the growth of Masonry along the Mother Lode, and the Fallon

House Theater, which once starred Lola Montez, Edwin Booth and Lotta Crabtree, now presents a summer repertory from the University of the Pacific. The huge gold scales in the Wells Fargo office weighed out over $55 million in dust and nuggets. The whole family can try their hand at panning on the Hidden Treasure Gold Mine Tour, tel. 532-9693; $1 for children, $1.50 for adults. There are stage coach rides, weekends in summer. The park museum offers exhibits on the Indians, the Chinese population (once one-sixth of Columbia) and, of course, the gold miners. Picnic spots are available, so plan to spend an enjoyable afternoon in this thriving ghost town.

Moaning Cave

Vallecito; (near Columbia State Historic Park; ask for directions). Tel. 736-2708. Daily 10 A.M.-5 P.M., May-Oct.; Wed.-Sun. in winter. Adults, $1.50; 11 & under $1.

● You can count the 144 winding steps that lead you 165 feet down to a graveyard of prehistoric bones and moaning winds. You'll see fantastic rock formations, such as Elephant's Ears, Giant Eagle, and the Little Girl's Face, that add to the eerie feeling that you're intruding on unknown spirits. Picnic tables and a wide view of the hills on both sides offer a pleasant waiting place, as does the museum waiting room. Stalactites hang "high" from the

The Sierra Railroad

ceiling and stalagmites are "mighty mounds" on the floor — that's how we remember which is which.

The Peppermint Stick

Main St., Murphys. Tel. 728-3570. Daily, afternoons and early evenings.

● San Andreas shakes, Sierra sodas, 49er parfaits, and Mercer Cavern Stalagmites head the menu of this nice old-fashioned soda parlor. Special sodas and sundaes like the Black Bart Treasure and the Mother Lode Banana Split are equally enticing. Home-made candies fill the counter shelves, and their heavenly aroma greets you when you open the door. If you're on the run, try a peppermint ice cream cone.

P.L. Travers Building & Old Timer's Museum

Main Street, Murphys. Daily, 10 A.M.-5 P.M., summer; weekends 10 A.M.-dusk, winter. Free.

● The P.L. Travers building, dating from 1856, houses both the museum and a rock shop. In the museum, spinning wheels, old clocks, a coffee mill and special carpenters' tools are some of the interesting Murphys memorabilia. Across the street is the Murphys Hotel, where Black Bart, Mark Twain, General Grant and Horatio Alger all spent some time. Photos and mementos of the guest celebrities are also shown in the museum. The Vern Hauselt Blacksmith Show, with old bellows and forge is also interesting.

Mercer Caverns

Ebbetts Pass Highway, Murphys. Tel. 728-2101. Daily, 9 A.M.-5 P.M., summer, weekends, 11 A.M.-4 P.M., winter. Adults, $1.75, ages 5-11, 75¢.

● This 30-minute tour past stalactites and stalagmites, aragonites and helictites takes you into a subterranean wonderland. Eerie rock formations like the Organ Loft, Angel Wings and the Chinese Meat Market are dazzling examples of the artistry of nature. Mercer Caverns was discovered in 1885 by a tired, thirsty prospector, Walter J. Mercer, who noticed bay bushes growing near a limestone bluff and thought he had found water.

Angels Camp Museum

753 Main St., Angels Camp. Tel. 736-2963. Daily ex. Tues., 9 A.M.-6 P.M., summer; weekdays, 1-5 P.M., weekends 10 A.M.-5 P.M., May; Thurs.-Mon., 10 A.M.-5 P.M., winter. Oct. Mon.-Fri. 10 A.M.-5 P.M.; Closed Tues. & Wed. in Nov. Adults, 50¢; ages 6-12, 25¢.

● Minerals, rocks, gemstones, hunks of quartz containing gold, are the main attractions here. You'll also find colorful maps of the Mother Lode and clothes, tools and other remnants of the golden years at Angels Camp. A rusty old fire engine, petrified wood, cave stalactites and exotic old machinery surround the building.

A few miles out of town, on the way to Columbia State Historic Park, you can peek into a replica of Mark Twain's cabin during his tenure on Jackass Hill in 1864-65. Here he gathered material for his *Jumping Frog of Calavaras County* and wrote *Roughing It*, the story that brought him fame.

Five miles north of Angels Camp at San Andreas is the Calaveras County Museum at 30 Main St. (open Mon., Wed., Fri., 10-5, Tues. and Thurs. 1-9, Sat. 1-4, free). Located on the second floor of one of San Andreas' vintage buildings, this small museum houses displays of minerals, old firearms, Indian relics and town documents.

Amador County Museum

225 Church St., Jackson. Tel. 223-0162. Daily ex. Tues., 12-4 P.M. Free.

● Household goods, musical instruments, baby things, stuffed animals, minerals, and, naturally, gold miners' tools are to be found in this excursion into the last century. The carriage house which holds a model of the Kennedy Mine, still a working mine, is also on the grounds.

One mile out North Main St., there are two wheels on either side of the road, 58' in diameter. They were used to transport waste from the mine. The *Jackson Trailing Wheels* are almost lost in our his-

tory, but their size is still impressive.

The Gold Rush Museum

Main Street, Amador. Tel. 267-0260. 10¢.

● An incredible working model of a gold mine is one of the leading attractions in this small museum. It shows all of the mine operations and was constructed by the miners 100 years ago. Indian and gold miners' artifacts are the main emphasis of the collection, with gold nuggets, old money, Indian baskets and toys used by the Indian and miners' children. The museum itself has been open to the public for about 100 years, and although it may be hard to locate, it's well worth another 100 years of support.

Chaw-Se Indian Grinding Rock State Historic Park

Pine Grove-Volcano Rd., Volcano. Tel. 296-4440. Open to visitors and campers daily, weather permitting. Day picnic use: $1.

● When you walk up to the top of the hill, all you see is a huge, flat rock with a few pockmarks and scratchy lines, surrounded by a wooden fence. Then you get closer and see that the scratchy lines are petroglyphs by the Miwok Indians to commemorate their tales of hunting and fishing. The pockmarks are actually mortar holes — 1,185 of them — in which the Indian women

Columbia SHP

ground the seeds, bulbs, fungi and acorns that served as the staple in the diet. Each of the mortar holes was abandoned when it became too deep. The acorn meal is sifted and washed many times to remove bitterness. Then the meal is mixed with water in a basket, into which hot rocks are dropped, to heat the mush. One family consumed 2,000 pounds of acorns a year! The limestone bedrock was where the women met to work and gossip. Miwok bark houses and a ceremonial roundhouse and corn granary are on view, and the local ranger is planning to add more.

Sam's Town

Cameron Park, Hwy. 80, Shingle Springs. Tel. 677-2273/933-1662. Restaurant: 6 A.M.-2 A.M. Fri. & Sat. Store & Museum: 9 A.M.-9 P.M. daily.

● What a perfect place to stop for a meal on your way to or from the Gold Country! Sam's is a town, restaurant and amusement park all in one. The "front" of the building looks like an old town, with doctor's office, stable, saloon and theater; but the inside is one large building divided into restaurants, a gift and book shop, a honky-tonk piano bar, a historical wax museum and a "Museum of American Nostalgia." The elegantly chandeliered Lillian Russell room serves steaks — ($8.95 top) and a variety of complete meals; the other dining spots, all with sawdust on the floor, are self-service with hamburgers, roast beef sandwiches and fried chicken as the

main fare. Lining all the walls are nickel and dime games and "movies" of the San Francisco earthquake, the Gay 90s and much more. Outside, buggies, surreys, covered wagons and chariots stand near two old "Whistlestop" railroad cars that dispense fast, fast food. With this ambiance, the food is rightfully secondary. Our kids had a ball.

Placerville

Chamber of Commerce 542 Main St., Placerville. Tel. 626-2344.

● Old Hangtown, named after the Hanging Tree in the center of town, is now the more dignified Placerville. A drive around town will illustrate its history. *The Pony Express Harness Shop* (3030 Sacramento St.) served as the Western terminus of the Pony Express in 1861 and, later, as the stage stop for California Stage Co. & Pioneer Stage lines. The *Wells Fargo Office* (362 Main St.) was the scene of many gold shipments; James Hume was stationed here when he brought Black Bart and his bandits to justice. *Placerville Hardware* (Main St.), built in 1854, houses one of the oldest continuing hardware businesses in the state. Nearby, the *Camino Narrow Gauge Railway* "Cable & Northern Railroad" runs on weekends from 11 to 5. The *Michigan-California Lumber Company* arranges tours which begin with uncut logs and end with lumber being loaded into freight cars.

Gold Bug Mine

Bedford Park, Placerville. Tel.
622-0832. Daily, 8 A.M.-dusk. Free.

● The only municipally owned,
open-to-the-public gold mine in the
world, the Gold Bug Mine was
worked as recently as 1947. The
longer shaft of the mine (1,362 feet)
ends at an exposed gold-bearing
quartz vein. Bare bulbs lighting the
wooden walkways catch the glitter
of gold in the walls and ceilings. The
occasional drip of water heightens
the cool, eerie silence of the tunnel.
The huge gold-stamp mill by the
creek is being restored. The park is
wild and rugged, with scattered
picnic facilities near the creek.

Ghost Mountain Ranch

Pollack Pines. Tel. 644-2415. Daily,
9 A.M.-5 P.M. in winter, 8:30 A.M.-7:30
P.M. in summer. Free. Picnic use:
Adults 75¢, children 50¢.

● Ghost Mountain Ranch is one of
the chain of Yogi Bear Jellystone
Park Campgrounds. It offers the
adventure of a Western ranch with
modern camping and swimming
facilities. Day visitors can stroll
through the Wells Fargo Office, the
jail, the post office and general
store, or visit an Indian Village, ride
a pony or stagecoach and join in a
Western barbecue. The $75,000
Western antique display is impressive and the gold mine and logger's
cabin are fun. "Puppet Place" gives
puppet shows for those over 3 years
old (30¢, or four for $1). The day we
visited the ranch, we saw a day-old
colt teetering around his mother.

Marshall Gold Discovery State Historic Park

Hwy. 49, Coloma. Tel. 622-3470.
Picnicking, $1 per car. Museum:
daily, 10 A.M.-5 P.M. adults, 25¢, ticket
usable at all state parks that day.

● Sutter's Mill has risen again on the
American River. The museum is
very modern, a complete exhibit of
the discovery of gold and the lives of
the gold miners. There are maps,
tools and relics from the miners, a
pictorial display of the discovery, an
exhibit of the Gold Rush routes and
a piece of timber from the first mill.
Gold dust and nuggets, geological
exhibits and the story of the Maidu
Indians are also displayed. On the
grounds an 1860 general store and
bank, a Chinese store and a stamp
mill are equipped and in working
order. The table in the Mormon
workers' cabin is set for dinner. The
miner's cabin is furnished (with a
huge tin of coffee, cans of beans and
a scale and Bible) right down to the
miner in bed with his boots on.
Another building houses models of
gold-mining methods. But the best
thing of all is to stand next to the big
wheel of the mill and look down on
the quiet river that changed history.
The ranger has been known to saw a
log or two in the mill at noon on
weekends.

Sierra Nevada House III

Hwy. 49, Coloma. Tel. 622-5856.

● The third Sierra Nevada House is
almost next to Marshall Gold Discovery State Park on Highway 49.
This old-fashioned hotel offers three

kinds of food. For proper meals and good thick steaks try the elegant 1880s dining room. The soda parlour serves breakfasts, snacks and sandwiches on marble tables with curly wire chairs. Or, if you're in a hurry, have an ice cream cone to go!

Placer County Historical Museum

Old Town, Auburn Fairgrounds, Pleasant Ave., Auburn. Daily ex. Mon., 10 A.M.-4 P.M., summer; weekends and holidays, 10 A.M.-5 P.M., winter. Free.

● Old mining equipment and pioneer mementos depict the early days of Placer County. Wagons, mineral samples, furniture and mannequins in antique clothing are features of the display. In nearby Old Town, antique shops, quaint old buildings and an old-fashioned, completely equipped firehouse are open for inspection and nostalgia.

North Star Mine Powerhouse

114 Mill St, at Empire, Grass Valley. Tel. 273-9853. 11 A.M.-5 P.M., Daily May-Oct., weekends in winter. Soon to be a State Park. 50¢.

● Built by A.D. Foote in 1875, this is the first complete water-powered, compressed-air transmission plant of its kind. The compressed air, generated by 10-ton, 30-foot Pelton water wheels, furnished power for the entire mine. The small, well-organized museum houses photos, ore specimens and small machinery, but the main attractions are the wheels, bridges and walkways of the building itself.

The homes of Lola Montez and Lotta Crabtree are on Mill Street. Lola was a Bavarian singer, dancer and king's favorite, who fled to the Gold Country in 1853, when her king fell from power. Lotta Crabtree, a young neighbor, became Lola's protege and soon became famous, rich and beloved throughout America. Lola's home is open to the public daily (12-4 P.M., free) during the summer. Mt. St. Mary's Museum on So. Church St., open 1-4 P.M., weekends, is also of interest.

In the center of Grass Valley, right in the central park, is the Empire Mine, one of the greatest hard-rock mines in California. Visitors are welcome here, and in the nearby Idaho-Maryland, North Star and Pennsylvania gold mines.

Firehouse #1 Cultural Museum.

214 Main St., Nevada City. Tel. 265-9941. Daily, 10:30 A.M.-4:30 P.M. Free.

● The Nevada Historical Society's museum houses Maidu baskets and artifacts and memorabilia of the county's first settlers. The Bicentennial museum annex is open 12-4 P.M. daily, upon request at the Fire use.

An American-Victorian museum-restaurant complex is now being completed in the Old Foundry on Spring Street by local proprietors Osborne & Weed.

Malakoff Diggins State Historic Park

North Bloomfield Tel. 265-2740. Mon.-Fri. 10 A.M.-4:30 P.M., 9 A.M.-6 P.M. weekends in summer. Sept. & June 10-5 weekends. Closed Oct. 1-May. Free.

• Many millions of dollars worth of gold poured from these huge hydraulic diggings, and a small sign informs visitors that there's still enough gold left here, and throughout the Gold Country, to mine $12 million worth annually for the next 50 years. The museum displays a model of the monitor used in the gold mines, showing how hydraulic mining worked. Photos of the 2-mile Bloomfield tunnel, the 12-foot-long skis used by miners, a portable undertaker's table, an 1870 stethoscope, mementos of the Chinese miners, and an old-time bar and poker room are some of highlights. Be prepared for the road to the Diggins, which is a long, twisting, narrow, hilly 17-mile drive out of Nevada City.

On the other side of the Malakoff Diggins, on Highway 49, is Downieville, a quiet Gold Rush town. Here you'll find the Sierra County Museum on Main Street (daily, 9:30 A.M.-4 P.M., May 1-Sept. 15 and by appt.; free) in one of the town's oldest stone buildings. Visitors will see gold mining tools, sample ores, and a variety of remembrances from the area.

Rough and Ready

• Driving from Grass Valley to Yuba City on Hwy. 20, you'll pass through a small town called Rough and Ready, the only town in the United States ever to name itself a nation. Rough and Ready seceded from the Union on April 7, 1850, and became known as "The Great Republic of Rough and Ready," with a president, a constitution, and its own flag. By July 4th, it had quietly slipped back into the United States. The garage owner we talked to said that the citizens returned to the fold because they couldn't get any liquor. Every year, the townspeople set aside the period of April 7 to July 4 to celebrate their short-lived independence.

Lake Tahoe

Visitors Center, Hwy. 89 So. Lake Tahoe, Tel. 541-0209.

• Lake Tahoe is world-famous for its crystal-clear water and beautiful surroundings. Visitors can ski, water-ski, boat, swim (only in August unless you like cold toes), sun, backpack and hike, or just relax and enjoy the forest wilderness. Naturalist programs are given on summer weekends in the D. L. Bliss and Emerald Bay State Parks and at Camp Richardson. Movies and shows are held in the Lake of the Sky Amphitheater. Tahoe Cruises, Wed.-Sat., from 8:45 A.M. (Info. at Visitors Center.)

Vikingsholm, a 38-room Nordic fortress, is open to the public daily in summer, 10-12 A.M. and 1-5 P.M., on Emerald Bay's southwest shore. You can boat right to the entrance to save yourself a hike.

The *Taylor Creek Stream Profile Chamber* (daily in summer, 9 A.M.-5 P.M.; Wed.-Sun., 10-4 in fall) near Camp Richardson is part of the El Dorado National Forest Visitors Center. You can take one of their free self-guided nature walks through a mountain meadow and marsh and down into the chamber, where you look through glass windows to see the rainbow trout and aquatic life of a naturally flowing mountain stream. Recorded messages help you identify the fish and plants in front of you.

The *Tahoe, Trout Creek and Pacific Railroad* (U.S. Hwy. 50, Al Tahoe Post Office, So. Lake Tahoe; June 14-Sept. 6, 10 A.M.-4:30 P.M. daily ex. Sun., adults $1.50; under 12, 75¢. The 20-minute ride on this newly restored narrow-gauge steam line passes the pockmarked Indian Rock, where Indians used to grind nuts into flour, pine forests, Trout Creek and the old logging railroad, the Lake Valley. The colorful 2-4-2 "Columbia" type locomotive once operated on a sugar plantation in Hawaii.

Donner Memorial State Park

(roads closed in winter) Donner Lake, Truckee. Tel. 587-3789. Daily, June 15-Labor Day, 9 A.M.-5 P.M. Weekends, 10 A.M.-noon & 1-4 P.M. during the rest of the year, when possible. Adults, 25¢.

● The Emigrant Trail museum combines natural history with one of the most dramatic of human stories. Man's conquest of the Sierra Nevada and the tragic story of the Donner party are told with relics, dioramas, pictures, and models. During the disastrous winter of 1846, a party of 89 tried to make it through the Sierras to California. Only 47 survived. The memorial to the Donner Party is 22 feet high, symbolic of the early 22-foot snowfall that trapped them. Chinese railroad workers, the "Big Four" railroad tycoons, miners and mountain men are also remembered in this small museum.

Plumas Eureka State Historic Park

Johnsville Star Route, Blairsden. Tel. 836-2380 Daily, 8 A.M.-5 P.M. Adults, 25¢

● An assay office and museum portray gold mining and pioneer life in the town of Johnsville.

12

THE REDWOOD COUNTRY

The Redwood Country is one of the most beautiful areas in America. Stately evergreens line the roads and the Pacific Ocean crashes into the shoreline. Some of the beaches are craggy and surrounded by dangerous currents. Others are calm and protected, with long empty stretches for solitary walks. You can dash up from San Francisco on Hwy. 101 or you can spend hours wending along the coastline on Hwy. 1. You can enjoy the Victoriana of Ferndale and Eureka or you can lose yourself in the tiny fishing villages of Rockport and Noyo. The waters may be too cold to swim in, but the fish thrive, and are there for the catching. The Redwood Country lets you set your own pace — there are many places to see and things to do close to each other, and there are enough parks and beaches for you to relax or picnic in, whenever the mood strikes. It's a perfect place for a weekend, or a week.

Redwood Forest

Point Arena Lighthouse

*Off Hwy. 1, Point Arena. Tel.
882-2292. Sat., Sun., and holidays,
1-4 P.M. Free.*

● This rebuilt U.S. Coast Guard
lighthouse is located just north of a
tiny seacoast town at the end of a
long jet of land. It's a magnificent
setting with the ocean slapping at
the rocks below and the rolling
evergreen mountains behind you.
Since there's nothing between you
and the ocean breeze, there's usually a chilling amount of it, so bring
along something warm. Inside the
fog signal building, the fog horn and
radio-beacon equipment are on display. Photos show what the original
lighthouse looked like before it was
destroyed in the 1906 earthquake.

Masonite Corp. Demonstration Forest.

*Hwy. 128 between Navaro & Little
River.*

● This 600-yard forest trail shows a
commercially grown forest. Points
of interest are well-marked. A display of how masonite is made and
used, from log leftovers, to chips, to
fiber, to blank board, to pressed
board, to panels is always available,
as is a nice picnic area.

Higabee Petting Zoo & Animal Farm

*18150 Ocean Drive, Ft. Bragg. Tel.
964-0466. 9:30 A.M. to dusk, daily in
summer; weekends in winter. Adults,
$1.50; Children, $1.*

Point Arena Light Station

● Animals roam in a pastoral setting
and everything's pettable including
lovable llamas and General
Mohammad, a bronze turkey. Children can feed the animals from an
animal-chow-filled ice cream cone,
check the pond for fish, and walk
along nature trails. If you've ever
wanted to pet a wallabie, peacock or
chinchilla, this is the place to head
for.

Mendocino

● Mendocino is an area of beautiful,
rocky beaches, a mecca for drift-
wood collectors, beachcombers,
and strollers. The town has appeared in many movies and there
are nice, interesting little streets to
browse along when it gets too foggy
for beachwalking. Among the highlights in town are: The *Mendocino
Art Center* (540 Little Lake St.; tel.
937-5819) offers changing exhibits
of the works of local artists. Films
and children's theater are

scheduled irregularly. The children especially liked the bright flying banners and colorful stained-glass windows. *The Soup Kitchen* (Kasten and Ukiah Sts.) offers hand-crafted toys and furniture and the *Ice Cream Place* offers cold delights. Down the block, the *Kelley House* (with Father Time chasing a lovely damsel on the roof) is being restored (phone 937-5791 for appt.).

Mendocino Coast Botanical Gardens

1822 No. Hwy. 1 Fort Bragg. Tel. 964-4352. Adults, $1.75; 13-18, $1.25; 6-12, 75¢ Daily, 8:30 A.M. to 6 P.M., (5 P.M. in winter.)

• Whole families of quail live in this flower-laden 47-acre forest and sea coast garden. Visitors walk through nurseries, beside twinkling brooks, over wooden bridges, and through canyons and dells out to the very edge of the ocean. A cliff house overlooks the sea-swept rocks. Most of the plants, flowers, and shrubs are discreetly identified, and if your garden needs brightening, the nursery at the entrance offers many plants at good prices.

Noyo Harbor

off Hwy. 1, Noyo.

• The Noyo River meets the sea just south of Fort Bragg and a large fishing fleet makes its home in this picturesque little haven. Visitors can dine on fresh fish in the modest restaurants while watching the boats return after a day of work. The kids will also like walking around the docks for a closer look at the boats.

Georgia Pacific Logging Museum

90 W. Redwood, Fort Bragg. Tel. 964-5651. Mon.-Fri., 8 A.M.-5 P.M. Free.

• Built in 1857 as the guest house for the Indian reservation army post, this small white house is now surrounded by huge, awe-inspiring machines that were used in the 1880s for hauling logs out of the forest and for skidding them onto the landing. A huge slide of redwood that was 1,753 years old in 1843 is also on display. Inside, historical pictures of the industry, huge bellows, mementos of the loggers, and ship's models complete the museum collection. Redwood films and a one-hour tour past the sawmill, debarker and lumber cutters in the mill accentuates the differences between the smooth industrial present and the rugged past. Nearby, at the foot of Walnut St., is the Georgia Pacific Nursery (8-4:30 weekdays) which holds 1.4 million redwood and Douglas fir seedlings. A display room explains reforestation and timber management. An arboretum, nature trails, and picnic tables are available. A free packet of redwood seeds is mailed to each visiting family.

The Skunk Railroad

The Skunk Railroad

California Western Railroad, Fort Bragg. Skunk Depot, Tel. 964-5651 Super Skunk Steam Train: daily, in summer leaves Ft. Bragg 10 A.M.; arrives Willits 12:40 P.M.; leaves Willits 2:25 P.M.; arrives Ft. Bragg 4:55 P.M. Also Sats., Apr. 29-May 20 and Sept. 16-Oct. 28. Skunk Diesel Rail Car: Daily, year round; leaves Ft. Bragg 9:50 A.M.; arrives Willits 11:55 A.M.; leaves Willets 1:50 P.M.; arrives Ft. Bragg 3:50 P.M. Skunk: Daily, in summer leaves Ft. Bragg 5:30 P.M. arrives Willits 7:30 P.M.; leaves Willits 7:15 A.M.; arrives Ft. Bragg 9:15 A.M. Adults: round-trip $8.20, one way, $5.45, ages 5-11, $4.10 and $2.75. Reservations advised.

● The Skunk Railroad should be a California landmark. During the exciting 40-mile trip from Fort Bragg to Willits, the train crosses 32 trestles and bridges, goes through two tunnels, and twists and turns over spectacularly curved track (at one point, one section of the track winds right above the one below). You travel through the quiet Noyo riverbed to high mountain passes and pastures and into the redwood forest. The bouncy diesel Skunk and the roaring Steam Super Skunk are both well worth the price and time. Reservations are advised (California Western RR, P.O. Box 907-B, Fort Bragg, 95437).

Far Far West Museum

358 S. Main St., Willits, Tel. 459-5580. Daily, 10 A.M.-5 P.M., May-Nov.; weekends 10 A.M.-3 P.M., winter. Adults, $1; students, 75¢; children, 25¢.

● If the Skunk Railroad leaves you in Willits with a few hours to pass, this museum is a nice way to do it. An old barber shop, country store, post office, bar, kitchen, pantry and harness and blacksmith shop are carefully reproduced to give visitors a picture of pioneer life in the area in the 1880s. Redwood products, a moonshiner's still, Indian arts and crafts and wildlife dioramas are also part of the collection.

Nearby, the *Mendocino County Museum* at 400 E. Commercial St., tel. 459-2736 (daily, 10 A.M.-4:30 P.M., in summer) is just getting organized. Historical articles and documents reflecting the history of Mendocino County have been gathered for this interesting collection.

Louisiana Pacific Demonstration Forest

Rte. #1 Rockport. Free.

● A quiet, 20-minute guided walk of 400 yards along a scenic creek provides a living demonstration of how the forest is cared for. You learn that only one percent of the tree is living — the tips of its roots, the leaves, buds, flowers, seed and a single thin layer of cells sheathing the tree. You see Douglas firs, white firs and redwood residuals — the redwood trees that have sprung up from seed and sprouts in three generations.

The Drive-Thru Tree

At the turnoff to Hwy. 1, Leggett. Tel. 925-6363. Daily, 9 A.M.-6 P.M., later in summer. Nominal entrance fee for day use.

● This large, chandelier-shaped, 315-foot redwood was tunneled in 1934 and a standard or large-sized contemporary car just fits through. We could touch both sides of the tree from the compact we were driving at the time. The winding dirt road leading to the tree takes you right to a little gift shop, and on to the highway. There are 200 acres of nature trails and picnic areas for you to use.

Confusion Hill

Hwy. 101, Piercy. Tel. 925-6456. Daily, 8:30 A.M.-6:30 P.M., April-Sept. Confusion Mysteries: Adults, $1; ages 6-12, 50¢. Mountain train: Adults, $1; ages 3-12, 50¢.

● The Mountain Train follows many switchbacks to take you 1¼ miles up to the summit of a redwood mountain, through a tunnel tree, and back down. Huckleberries, tanoak, madrone trees and small creatures abound in this wilderness despite the daily incursions of the squeaking, whistling train. Back at the bottom of the mountain, try the other experience at Confusion hill — a spot where gravity is defied and your eyes tell lies. You seem to be standing sideways and water seems to run uphill. Your companions may shrink or grow taller even though you're standing on a level plane.

Marbles and bottles appear to roll uphill. Nobody knows why all of this happens, but the kids are delighted by it.

Avenue of the Giants

Humboldt Redwoods State Park, Weott. Tel. 946-2311.

● Besides being one of the few tree species to have survived from the time of the dinosaurs, the redwoods are awesome, beautiful trees to behold. A leisurely drive down the Avenue of the Giants leads you to a protected wilderness of massive, soaring trees and moss-and-fern-carpeted landscape occasionally spotted with deer. Founder's Grove, Rockefeller Forest and, naturally, Children's Forest, are some of the best of the special redwood groves.

Pacific Lumber Company

Scotia, Tel. 764-2222. Free museum and mill tours daily. Mon.-Fri.

● Scotia is an old logging town that was built entirely of redwood. The museum, a fine old mansion, presents pictures of the loggers at work and play and a collection of logging equipment, tools and relics. The self-guided tour through the mill takes about an hour and follows the processing of a log from the moment it comes off the truck. The first step is one of the most impressive — a debarker that uses water pressure to peel the log like a banana (up until 10 years ago, men did the de-barking with a crowbar). Many things go on all at once in the mill, and our kids got completely carried away by the place.

Clendenen's Cider Works

12th St., Fortuna. Tel. 725-2123.

● Work at the cider mill begins early in the morning, Monday-Friday, August to January. If the crop is very heavy, the mill will see action until the afternoon and even on weekends. Monday and Thursday are pressing days. Throughout the year, you can buy cold, delicious cider by the cup, half gallon ($1.10), and gallon ($1.70). A frozen gallon will keep for at least two days in the trunk of your car until you can get home to a refrigerator.

Alton & Pacific Railroad

Hwy. 36, ½ mile east of Hwy. 101, Alton. Wed.-Sun., 11 A.M.-6 P.M. on the hour. Adults, 75¢ ages 5-15, 50¢. 15-minute train ride.

● The Alton & Pacific Railroad is the only known 2-foot narrow-gauge-wood-burning steam train on the Pacific Coast. A ride on this rattling old train is a must for train buffs of any age.

Clarke Memorial Museum

Third and E. Sts. Eureka. Tel. 433-1947, Tues.-Sat., 10 A.M.-4 P.M.; Sun. 1-4 P.M.; closed Sun. and Mon. in winters. Free.

● This large old-fashioned pioneer and natural history museum is stuffed with fascinating collections. Animal heads and 1,300 stuffed birds, as well as the largest collection of birds' eggs (2,635) we've ever seen, attract youngsters. Indian baskets, several gun collections, ships' bells, and old typewriters and sewing machines also get their share of attention. There are over 100 antique American, Chinese, and Japanese dolls. Western Americana and mementos of early Humboldt County life round out this impressive presentation.

Fort Humboldt S.H.P.

3431 Fort Ave., Eureka. Tel. 433-4588. Daily, 8 A.M.-5 P.M. Free.

● High on a windy hill overlooking a modern logging facility, Fort Humboldt is mainly an outdoor museum of the logging industry. Old machinery is accompanied by large billboards telling the visitor what it was like to be a logger in the 19th century. A logger's cabin is furnished with a stove, a bed, a shelf of beans and beef and a 19th-century "girly" calendar. You learn how to "fall" a tree, then see how to drag it out of the forest and cut it up. An 1884 Falk locomotive and an 1892 Andersonia locomotive are on view behind glass windows. Nearby is old Fort Humboldt, where U.S. Grant served as a staff officer in the 1850s. The small museum shows powderhorns, bullet molds and uniforms dating to the original fort, as well as pictures of the Tolowa, Hoopa and Yurok Indians who lived in the area. Restoration of the fort and enlargement of the museum is now under way.

Samoa Cookhouse

Samoa Road, Eureka. Tel. 442-1659. Breakfast: 6-11 A.M., a la carte lunch: 11 A.M.-2 P.M.; Adults, $2.00; ages 7-11, $1.00; ages 3-6, 55¢. Dinner: 5-10 P.M.; Adults, $3.75; ages 7-11, $1.85; ages 3-6, 95¢.

● Family-style meals are served seven days a week in this original lumbercamp cookhouse which once served as relief quarters for shipwreck victims. The long tables are set as they were in 1900, with red and white checked cloths and large bottles of catsup. The night we were there, dinner consisted of clam chowder, roast beef *and* turkey, potatoes, vegetables, salad, relishes, and hot apple pie. Tasty home-baked bread goes with everything, and you can buy a loaf (55¢) for tomorrow's picnic. Before or after your meal, wander through the adjoining rooms and see the assemblage of loggers' boots, dinner bells, old kitchen implements, photos of the logging trains, and a steam coffee maker that served 500 men three times a day.

Patrick's Point S.P.

Trinidad. Tel. 677-3570. Daily, 10-4. Park entrance fee $1 per car.

● Two small cases of Yurok artifacts, natural history exhibits, geology and rock displays are located at park headquarters.

Humboldt State University Marine Laboratory

Trinidad. Tel. 677-3671. Mon.-Fri., 8 A.M.-5 P.M.; Sat. and Sun., 12-5 P.M. Free.

● Located at Land's End, in the picturesque fishing village of Trinidad, this working laboratory is open to the public for self-guided tours. Hallway aquariums hold both rare and common molluscs and crustaceans and fresh-and-salt-water fish. Shovel-nose catfish, Siamese Tiger fish, buffalo sculpins, red, white and green anemones and walleye surfperches look over their visitors. In one tank, a 3½-foot wolf eel has been trained to eat out of a man's hand and in another, a small black octopus goes through behavioral experiments to see if she can distinguish different shapes and patterns.

Do stop at the *Trinidad Lighthouse* on your way to the laboratory. This is the spot where the Spaniards landed on Trinity Sunday in 1775. Although the coal lantern of the lighthouse was replaced in 1947, the original gear system of descending weights is still working to turn the light. The original 2-ton bell, now replaced by an air horn, is displayed in front.

Prairie Creek Fish Hatchery

Highway 101, Orick. Tel. 488-2253. Daily, 8 A.M.-5 P.M. Free.

● Just south of Prairie Creek State Park, this fish hatchery raises King Chinook and Coho salmon, and steelhead trout. The only county-owned hatchery in California, Prairie Creek offers a nice rest stop on the road between Crescent City and Eureka.

Prairie Creek Redwoods State Park

Highway 101, near Orick. Tel. 488-2861. Daily, 9 A.M.-5 P.M. Free.

• Roosevelt elk roam this state park and can usually be seen grazing across the meadow from the Visitors Center. A small but interesting exhibit on the elk and the trees, ferns, flowers and small animals of the area is on display in the Visitors Center, along with a small gold-mining exhibit and an old moonshiner's still. But the most extraordinary object in the exhibit is a madrone tree that grew to envelop the skull of an elk.

Klamath Jet Boat Kruises

Hwy. 101, 1 mi. north of Klamath. Tel. 482-4191. Leaves boat dock 9 A.M., daily in summer, returns 3 P.M. Adults, $8; ages 4-11, $4. Reservations advisable. (P.O. Box 5, Klamath, CA 95548).

• Skimming over the Klamath River on a jet-boat is an exciting experience. Deer, raccoon, bear and other animals are often spotted on the riverbank, and the rock formations surrounding the river make this 64-mile trip truly memorable. Hoopa Indians can be seen living with their age-old customs. Lunch is taken deep in Hoopa Indian ter-

ritory. Local Indian handiwork, particularly baskets, is on display.

Klamath and Hoppow Valley Steam Railroad

Terwer Valley offramp on Hwy. 101, at north end of Klamath Ridge Bridge, Klamath. Tel. 482-2533. Train departs every hour during the day, June through September. Adults, $1.50; under 12, 75¢.

• This 45-minute, 4-mile, open-air trip takes you to the top of the ridge overlooking the Klamath River. Pulled by one of two different logging engines — one a Minerets-type locomotive, the other a three-truck Heisler-geared locomotive — you'll travel along Hoppow Creek and pass the Peterson and Simpson sawmills. You have a choice of riding on an open flat car or on the caboose. Picnic areas are available.

Trees of Mystery

Hwy. 101, Klamath. Tel. 482-5613. Daily, 7:30 A.M.-7:30 P.M.; Sat. 7 A.M.-10 P.M., summer; daily, 8 A.M.-5 P.M., winter.

• Paul Bunyan, all 49 feet and 30,000 pounds of him, greets you at the entrance. Then you walk through a hollowed redwood log into a forest of redwoods, where recorded music and explanations take you to special trees like "The Family Tree," "The Fallen Giant" and the immense, moving "Cathedral Tree" at the top of the hill. Going back down the hill, you reach the best part from the children's point of view — Paul Bunyan and his "Trail of Tall Tales." You hear the wild stories of how Bunyan found Babe the Blue Ox, how the Grand Canyon was dug and how Sourdough Sam makes pancakes (his recipe includes the lard from one summer-fatted bear). The gift shop has an excellent museum of Indian artifacts and stocks a large and inviting selection of gifts, including redwood burls, pine-scented pottery, mountain cookbooks and Indian dolls.

Undersea Gardens of Crescent City

Anchor Way, Crescent City. Daily 9 A.M.-8 P.M., May-Oct. 15. Closed Oct. 15-May 1. Adults, $1.75; students, $1.25; ages 6-12, 75¢. Group rates available.

● Over 5,000 marine specimens live in this habitat 10 feet below sea level. You'll see ferocious wolf eels, scurrying crabs, sun starfish, and black snappers that stand vertically to aid their digestion. Sables (shark lookalikes) and lots of other unusual creatures swim, eat, and rest as if people weren't looking at them. A skin diver regularly gives lectures and demonstrations from the bottom. Lectures by Aquamaid are fun, too.

The McNulty Pioneer Home

7th & H Streets, Crescent City. Tel. 464-3922. Mon.-Sat., 1-4 P.M. Free.

● This charming 19th-century redwood house was a wedding present. A handsome carved bedroom set and baby's cradle, a bass mandolin piano and a sewing machine (that sewed material and leather) give the house a lived-in look. We were also impressed with the organ that came around the Horn in 1846, a huge French cherrywood armoire, a carved rosewood 16th-century Italian chair and pictures made with duck's down and seashells. Youngsters will be attracted to the picture of Victor, a red setter. Victor's mistress used to send him to the store with money and a shopping list in a basket and he would carry the groceries home to her.

Del Norte Historical Society Museum

640 H St., Crescent City. Tel. 464-3922 Wed.-Sat. 10-noon. Free.

● The 1935 version of *Last of the Mohicans* was filmed in Crescent City and this museum, once the county jailhouse, has many photos of the Indians who appeared in it. The most significant items in the collection include a model of a Yurok Indian bark house, stick games, headdresses, beads, dolls and baskets of the Tolowa, Pomo, Hoopa and Yurok tribes, and many Eskimo artifacts. Photos of Crescent City since its beginnings, with lots of "before and after" shots of the 1964 tidal wave, fill a hanging album. One room holds unicycles and a replica of an early steam donkey used in logging; another features a copy of the November 9,

1904, *San Francisco Examiner* proclaiming "Teddy Roosevelt is President!" Upstairs, in the old jail cells, are World War I uniforms, old radios and an entire blacksmith shop.

Battery Point Lighthouse

Crescent City. Daily ex. Fri., at low tide. Free.

● Battery Point Lighthouse is lo-cated offshore from Crescent City on a little island accessible only at low tide. The original light is still workable and the old log book, an antique banjo clock and several shipwreck photos and relics are on display. Although the children had high hopes that we would be stranded by the tide, the walk across the rocky beach to the mainland was blessedly uneventful.

Public Relations Tours

Crown Simpson Pulp Company

Fairhaven, Tel. 433-9771.

● Free tours, weekdays, 11 A.M. and 1 P.M., summer (children over 8 only). Phone for appt. in winter. Huge piles of woodchips are ground into pulp in this almost totally automated plant, in which visitors view the process from high, steep stairways. The half hour tour is followed by a 45-minute slide show that explains everything you've seen.

Simpson Timber Company, Mad River Plywood Mill

Arcata Alliance Rd., Blue Lake. Tel. 822-0371. Free tours, weekdays. 10 A.M. and 1:30 P.M.

● This half hour tour follows the log from forest to plywood press.

Simpson Timber Company Demonstration Forest

Highway 299, Blue Lake. Daily, daylight hours, May-Sept.

● Free demonstration of industrial forest management. Visitors walk through the forest reading plaques and learning how the forest is preserved and "farmed."

Mad River State Fish Hatchery

Blue Lake. Tel. 822-0592. Daily, 8 A.M.-5 P.M., June, July, and Aug.

● Salmon and steelhead fish eggs, baby fish and fingerlings may be seen in their holding tanks by the drop-in visitor. In Oct.-March view spawnings of adult salmon and steelhead. By the way, the river was named "mad" because of a fight between Joe Gregg and L.K. Wood, two explorers of the region in 1849, not because it's a ferocious river.

The Arcata Redwood Company's Mill "A" just north of Orick at Bald Hills Road Junction, welcomes visitors to view operations from overhead "catwalks."

13

NORTH CENTRAL CALIFORNIA

The North Central and Northeastern regions of California seem to be the most geographically ravaged parts of the state. The Lava Beds National Monument, Modoc National Forest, and Lassen Volcanic National Park are blastingly hot in summer and snowed-in in winter. Roads are infrequently traveled, and distances between towns are long. Overnight lodging should be arranged before you set out. At the same time, nature lovers will enjoy the Whiskeytown-Lake Shasta-Trinity area and all the wonderful open spaces whose very inaccessibility make them places to aim for.

Community Memorial Museum

1333 Butte House Rd., Yuba City. Tel. 674-0461. Tues.-Fri. 11-5 Free.

● This small community museum houses artifacts and remembrances of the Indians and early pioneers of Sutter County, as well as exhibits on the natural history of the area. Baskets and beads, grinding pots, and a skeleton represent the local Indians, while antique pianos lugged around Cape Horn, family books and Bibles and everyday clothing and dishes depict pioneer life. Mementos of the Chinese settlers

The Bidwell Mansion

are also included. But the starring item in the collection is Lola Montez' dressing table, surely one of the "tools" of this dazzling actress and seductress.

In Marysville, Yuba's Sister City, an 1856 family residence has become a museum, the *Mary Aaron Memorial Museum* at 704 D Street (Tues.-Sat., 1:30-4:30 P.M., free) with the original furniture and clothing and an interesting display of dolls, documents and photographs. Pioneer guns and mining and farming equipment are also shown.

Oroville Chinese Temple

1500 Broderick, Oroville. Tel. 533-1496. Mon. and Tues. 10-12 A.M. and 1-4:30 P.M. Wed. and Thurs. 1-4:30 P.M. Fri.-Sun. 10-12 A.M. and 1-4:30 P.M. Adults, $1; tours of 15 or more, 75¢ each.

• This complex of Buddhist, Taoist and Confucian temples houses one of the finest collections of Chinese artifacts in America. At the door of one building stands a two-ton cast-iron urn, given to the temple by Emperor Quong She. Carved teakwood altars, old tapestries, gods and goddesses, dragons, rare lanterns and shrines are found throughout the buildings. The Moon Temple, used for Buddhist worship, is entered through a circular doorway which symbolizes the circle of life. The arts and lives of the thousands of Chinese who migrated to the gold fields are wonderfully reflected in this peaceful spot.

Your admission ticket for the temple also allows you to visit the *Lott House Museum* at 1607 Montgomery St. (open Fri.-Tues. 10 A.M.-noon and 1-4:30 P.M.). Once the home of Judge C.F. Lott, this 19th-century house is furnished with period pieces and early American art.

Feather River Fish Hatchery and Oroville Dam

5 Table Mt. Blvd., Oroville. Tel. 534-2465/2324. Hatchery: Daily, 8 A.M.-6 P.M. Dam overlook 534-2330. 8 A.M.-9 P.M. May-Sept.; 8 A.M.-8 P.M., Oct. and Nov.; 8 A.M.-5 P.M.; Dec.-Apr. Free.

• A large window in the hatchery enables visitors to see the salmon climb the fish ladder to spawn (usually in September). Over 10,000 salmon and steelhead make their homes here now. 10 miles down the road, you can get a good view of the construction of the 770-foot dam across the Feather River.

Bidwell Mansion

Chico State College, 525 Esplanade, Chico. Tel. 895-6144. Daily, ex. holidays 10 A.M.-5 P.M. Adults, 25¢.

• Rancho Chico, covering 26,000 acres, was purchased in 1849 by agriculturist and politician John Bidwell. His large Victorian home soon became the social and cultural center of the upper Sacramento Valley. Bidwell's is a California success story. His first job was as clerk for John Sutter, then majordomo, and soon an officer in the Mexican War. After that, he set himself up at Chico and built a model farm. He raised corn, oats, barley, peaches, pears, apples, figs, quince, almonds, walnuts, sugar cane, olives and casaba melons. He was elected state senator and congressman, and even ran for President. Visitors may walk through the graciously furnished rooms, among which the library with its wicker sidechairs, tea cart, unique fireplace screen and weaving table, is special. We also liked a cabinet of stuffed birds in the General's office and the intricate Victorian hair wreaths in the parlor. The nearby Bidwell Park, third largest municipal park in the nation, was also part of the Bidwell estate. The park extends from Iron Canyon to the foothills of the Sierra Nevada and borders the sparkling Big Chico Creek. Picnic and play areas, hiking, bicycle and equestrian trails abound.

South Shasta Lines

Humann Ranch, Tehama Rd., Gerber. Tel. 385-1389. Open even numbered years in May and April on Sun. 1-4 P.M. by appt. Adults $2; under 12, $1.

● Fire boxes glow in the locomotives and the mailman catches mailbags tossed from a speeding train. Signs blink, bells ring, and railroad fans sigh nostalgically as the miniature 0-gauge wood-burning engine toots along. Twelve steam locomotives and 90 cars, all built to scale, operate along 820 feet of track. A railroad museum and old-time farm machinery display is open. On odd numbered years, there's a Steam Threshing Bee, Labor Day weekends.

William B. Ide Adobe

1 mile north of Red Bluff on Adobe Rd. Tel. 527-5927. Daily. 8 A.M.-5 P.M. Free.

William Ide Adobe

● "He hereby invites all good and patriotic citizens in California to assist him — to establish and perpetuate a liberal, a just and honorable government, which shall secure to all civil, religious and personal liberty." So wrote William B. Ide to introduce the Bear Flag Republic to California. When that idea failed, he went to the gold fields and then eventually returned home to his adobe, which also served as a ferry station between Sacramento and Shasta's Northern Gold Mines. The house is small and unassuming, with family photos, cradle and high chair, a furnished kitchen and an unusual sleeping platform under the eaves. A smokehouse and a carriage house, with covered wagons, buggies and Mr. Ide's branding equipment, are also open to the public. Two 300-year-old oaks lead the way to another small museum that includes gold-mining tools, an old button collection and a well-used cribbage board.

In town, the *Kelly-Griggs House Museum* (311 Washington St., 527-1129) is open for old house buffs, 2-5, Thurs.-Sun.

Shasta Dam

Hwy. 15, off Interstate 5. Tel. 275-1554/241-6584. June-Labor Day, 9-6, daily; 8:30-4 daily in winter. Free.

● Deer come to be fed by children when the lights shine on Shasta Dam at night. During the day, the 602-foot dam, the second highest in the world, is an even more spec-

tacular sight. Snow-capped Mount Shasta looms in the distance to accentuate the differences of natural and man-made wonders. A self-guided tour and a model and film tell you how the dam works. Jet-boat tours, houseboating, and every kind of water sport are popular in this Whiskeytown-Shasta-Trinity National Recreation Area.

Red Bluff Diversion Dam & Spawning Facility

Williams Ave. & Sale Lane, Red Bluff. Tel. 527-7440. Free.

● The world's largest artificial salmon-spawning channel is taking shape now near Red Bluff. Closed-circuit cameras, open to the public 16 hours a day, watch the fish moving through the channels of the facility. An interpretive center will soon be open from 8 to 4 daily. Movies on the migrating Chinooks will be shown and a glass viewing wall for watching the salmon will be provided. Another closed circuit TV to see the fish as they traverse the fish ladder is in the works. Salmon runs are heaviest from Oct. to Mid-Dec. Fish trapping and selecting activities may be observed at TV plaza area.

Fish hatchery buffs might like to ride to Anderson, 6 miles off Hwy. 5, above Red Bluff, to see the *Coleman National Fish Hatchery.* 365-8622, daily, 8 A.M.-4:30 P.M., free. Every year, 39 to 40 million salmon and steelhead eggs are hatched, then raised to catchable size in this hatchery. Spawning takes place in the fall, but there's always something to see here.

Redding Museum & Art Center

Caldwell Park, 1701 Rio Dr. Redding. Tel. 243-4994. Daily ex. Mon., 10 A.M.-5 P.M., summer; Tues.-Fri., noon-5 P.M., weekends, 10 A.M.-5 P.M., winter. Free.

● A fantastic doll collection — featuring a Shirley Temple doll, an 1850 papier-maché doll, a 1904 tin doll and 1908 *Ladies' Home Journal* paper dolls — is just one of the revolving exhibits shown in this small, excellent museum. There are changing monthly art shows and historical exhibits. The story of Pomo Indian basketry from birth (cradle), to home (pots, dress, luggage, the houses themselves), to death (gifts for the pyre) is remarkable. The permanent Indian and primitive collections include pre-Columbian pottery and figures, canoe prows from the Trobriand Islands and "wife beaters" from the Australian aborigines. Crafts, artifacts and baskets from the Hoopa, Karok, Yurok, Plains, Northwest Coast, Pomo, Zuni, Yaqui and Hopi Indians are nicely presented.

Shasta, Queen of the North

State Historic Park, Hwy. 299 west from Redding, Old Shasta. Tel. 243-8194. Daily, 10 A.M.-5 P.M. Adult ticket, 2ు , usable at all state parks the same day.

● Once the center of the rich Northern Gold Mines, Shasta is now a quiet ghost town in ruins. The old county courthouse and jail are well worth visiting for the displays of photographs and relics of the Indians, Chinese, gold miners and pioneers who once lived here. Modoc handicrafts, Chinese wooden pillows and money swords, an 1879 *Godey's Ladies Book* and the pistol John Brown used in his raid at Harper's Ferry are a few of the highlights of the collection. The courtroom is furnished as it was when in use and the jail downstairs is still equipped with chains, leg irons and a gallows outside. The courthouse also contains a remarkable collection of California art.

Weaverville Joss House State Historic Park

Hwy. 299W, Weaverville, Tel. 623-5284. Daily, ex. holidays, 10 A.M.-5 P.M. Adult ticket, 25¢, usable at all state parks the same day.

● The Temple of the Forest and the Clouds is open for worship as it has been since 1853. A small museum displays Chinese art, mining tools, weapons used in the tong wars and photos of Chinese Laborers building the railroads. A Lion Dance headdress, an abacus, opium pipes and a huge gong are also shown. Inside the temple, you see the paper money that is burned for the gods and the drum and bell that wake the gods so they'll hear your prayers. In the rear of the temple, the attendants' quarters are furnished as they were 100 years ago, with bunk beds and wooden pillows. Colorful altars, temple saints, celebration drums and flags and the mirror-covered king's umbrella that guarded him against evil spirits create a vivid picture of the religion and its people.

Trinity County Museum

Main St. (Hwy. 299W), Weaverville. Tel. 623-5211. Daily, 9 A.M.-5 P.M., May-Nov. Free.

• Right up the street from the old Joss House is this fine assemblage of historical mementos left by Weaverville's gold-mining pioneers. Household goods, guns, photographs, toys and dolls and an 1840 fire wagon are all well displayed. There is also an interesting exhibit on the Chinese tong wars and weapons. A reconstructed jailhouse and blacksmith shop help to recall this bygone era.

Lake Shasta Caverns

Off Lake Shasta, O'Brien. Tel. 238-2341. Tours throughout the day from 8 A.M., May-Sept; at 10 A.M., noon, and 2 P.M., winter. Adults, $3.50; ages 3-12, $1.75.

• Discovered in 1878 by J. A. Richardson (you can still see his inscription), the Lake Shasta Caverns are a natural wonder. Stalactite and stalagmite formations range from the 8-inch high "Ballerina" to the 60-foot high "Cathedral Room" of stalactite draperies studded with crystals. Multicolored formations

unfold before you during your tour, as you hear fact and Wintu Indian legend from a knowledgeable guide.

Siskiyou County Museum

910 So. Main St., Yreka. Tel. 842-3836. Daily ex. Mon. and holidays, 9 A.M.-5 P.M. Sunday 1-5 P.M. Summer, 9-5 daily. Free.

• The story of Siskiyou County is told in seven periods — Prehistoric, Indian, Trapper, Gold Rush, Transportation, Industry and Progress. The building itself is a reproduction of the old Callahan Ranch Hotel (1854), the first stage stop in the county. Silver, dishes, dolls, photographs, diaries and clothing of the pioneers are on the mezzanine. The basement displays a completely furnished country store, a miner's cabin, a milliner's shop and gun, mineral and Indian exhibits. Tree fossils, relics from the Hudson's Bay trappers and the huge shell of the eupachydiscus shellfish, 60 million years old, are of special interest.

Nearby, the *County Court House* at 4th and Lane Sts. (842-3531, Mon.-Fri., 8 A.M.-5 P.M.) displays gold nuggets, panned gold, placer gold and local gemstones.

Lava Beds National Monument

Off Hwy. 139, enter from Perez or Tule Lake. Tel. 667-2601. Information desk, with small museum, open 8 A.M.-9 P.M., June 15-Labor Day; 8 A.M.-5 P.M. the rest of the year. Camping $2 a night (summer only, bring supplies).

● Natural and Indian history vie for the visitor's attention in this monumental landscape created by black lava from the earth's crust. The area abounds with natural wonders: cinder cones reach up as high as 500 feet. Lava running underground has shaped hundreds of caves which can be explored. The Merrill Ice Caves contain a still river and a waterfall formed of ice. Fern Cave, named for the ferns it sustains, is decorated with drawings by the Indians who once lived here. You'll also find prehistoric Indian inscriptions carved into the bluffs overlooking Tule Lake. Captain Jack's Stronghold, a fort fashioned out of lava, is a grim reminder of later history: in 1872, Captain Jack led a band of Modoc Indians in a bloody but unsuccessful uprising against the U.S. Cavalry. A surprisingly wide variety of plant and animal life can also be enjoyed in this rocky landscape. Altogether, it's a fun place for the whole family if the weather is not too hot or cold.

Roops' Fort

75 N. Weatherlow St., Susanville. Tel. 257-5721. Daily, 10 A.M.-4 P.M. May 15-Oct. 15. Free.

● Governor of the Provisional Territory of Nevada and Nataqua, Isaac Roops named the city of Susanville after his daughter. Roops' Fort, built in 1854, was the first building in Lassen County. Nearby, the William H. Pratt Memorial Museum is filled with relics and artifacts of the natives, and the first settlers, Isaac Roops and Peter Lassen. An old stamp mill is on the grounds.

Lassen Volcanic National Park

Hwy. 36, Mineral. Tel. 595-4444. Info. Center at Manzanita Lake. Road closed in winter.

● Caves, hot springs, boiling pools, mud pots, sparkling lakes and the cinder cone which erupted in 1851 are visitor attractions in this lovely park. An Indian lore program at park headquarters, during the summer, tells the history and customs of the Yana, Yahi, Mountain Maidu and Atsugewi Indians who once camped here. Ishi, story-book hero and last man of the Yahi tribe, was found near here and the photos of him living with his customs in a modern world are really interesting. Indians of the other tribes still sell baskets and tell stories on the campgrounds. One note of warning: The ground in the thermal areas can give way at any time, and the hot pools have been known to kill, so keep hold of your children at all times. Lassen Peak erupted only 50 years ago and the natives are sure it will go off again, soon.

Public Relations Tours

Pacific Coast Producers

Oroville. Tel. 533-4311. Free tours (by appt.) in Aug. and Sept.

● See the former Stokely-Van Camp Company can fruit cocktail, peaches, pickles, and tomatoes.

Libby Cannery

100 Virginia St., Gridley. Tel. 846-5621. Free tours (by appt.).

● Libby cans peaches in July and August and pumpkin in September.

Lindsay Olive Growers

981 Fig Lane and 2nd St., Corning. Tel. 824-5444. Free tours (by appt.), Mon.-Fri., 8-12 A.M., 1-5 P.M.

● No tasting here, but an interesting tour.

SPECIAL ANNUAL EVENTS

January

San Francisco Sports and Boat Show, Cow Palace
San Mateo Auto Show, Fairgrounds
Harlem Globe Trotters, Coliseum, Oakland
Golden Gate Kennel Club All-Breed Dog Show, Cow Palace, San Francisco
Four Dog Sled Races, Prosser Lake and Donner Lake

February

Chinese New Year Celebration and Parade, San Francisco
Athens Track Meet, Coliseum, Oakland
National Road Show, Coliseum, Oakland
Crab Festival, Crescent City (first weekend)
Crab Cioppino Feasts, Bodega Bay, (first Sunday)
Cloverdale Citrus Fair (George Washington's Birthday weekend)
Chinese Bomb Day, Bok Kai Festival, Marysville
Clam Beach Run, Trinidad

March

Sierra Dog Sled Races, Sierra City, Truckee and Ebbetts Pass
Candlefishing at Night, Klamath River
Junior Grand National Livestock Exposition, Cow Palace, San Francisco (or early April)
Jackass Mail Run, Porterville (or first weekend in April)
Cherry Blossom Festival, Japantown, San Francisco (or 1st weekend in April)
Fortuna Antique Show & Sale

April

"Log Race," Petaluma River
San Francisco Giants Baseball, Candlestick Park (until Sept.)
Oakland A's Baseball, Oakland Coliseum (until Sept.)
Annual Crab Feed, Trinidad
Gem and Mineral Show, Cow Palace, San Francisco
Yacht Parade, Redwood City
Oakland Hobby Show
Carmel Kite Festival
Gold Nugget Days, Paradise, (third weekend)

Red Bluff Roundup and Rodeo (third weekend)
Coalinga Water Festival (third weekend)
Apple Blossom Festival, Sebastopol
Fresno Folk Festival (fourth weekend)
Rhododendron Festival, Eureka
Boonville Buck-A-Roo Days

May

Latin American Fiesta, Mission District, San Francisco
Opening Day Yacht Parade and regattas each weekend, San Francisco Bay
Ferndale Arts Festival
Ave. of the Giants Marathon, Garberville
Luther Burbank Rose Festival & Parade, Santa Rosa
San Francisco Ballet, Opera House
Mountain Open Air Play, Mt. Tamalpais State Park, Marin County (second weekend)
Jumping Frog Contest, Angels Camp, Calavaras, Sonora Fairgrounds (third weekend)
West Coast National Antique Fly-In, Watsonville Airport
Salinas Valley Fair, King City
Old Settlers Day, Campbell
Chamarita Festival and Parade, Half Moon Bay (Pentecost Sunday)
Chamarita Fete and Portuguese Feast, Sausalito (Pentecost Sunday)
Fireman's Muster, Columbia Ghost Town, (first weekend)
Lamb Derby Days, Willows (first Thursday)
Stump Town Days and Russian River Rodeo, Guerneville
Coarsegold Rodeo, Madera County
Fiddletown Gold Country Hoedown
Disney on Parade, Coliseum, Oakland
Hobby Fair, San Mateo Fairgrounds
V.F.W. White Water Boat Races, Willow Creek

June

Stumptown Days, Guerneville

Upper Grant Avenue Street Fair, San Francisco
Fly-In and Moonlight Flight, Porterville
Alameda Country Fair, Pleasanton
Merienda, Monterey's birthday party
San Antonio Mission Fiesta, Jolon
Springfest, San Mateo Fairgrounds
Old Auburn Flea Market
Italian Picnic and Parade, Sutter Creek
Shasta Brigade Jamboree, Redding
Malakoff Home-Coming, Nevada City
Solano County Fair, Vallejo
Novato County Fair
Pony Express Days, McKinleyville
Garberville Rodeo & Western Celebration
San Francisco Kite Festival
Bear Flag Day, Sonoma
Tuolumne Jubilee, Tuolumne City
Days of Kit Carson, Jackson
Middletown Days
Bonanza Days, Gilroy
Redwood Acres Fair, Eureka
Sonoma Marin Fair, Petaluma
Gun, Coin, Antique Collectors Hobby Show, Monterey
Western Daze, Fairfield, Suisun
Klamath Salmon Festival, Klamath River
Western Weekend and Rodeo, Novato (first weekend after school)
Swedish Festival, Kingsburg, (second Saturday)
Vaquero Days, Hollister (June 18)
Horse Show and Rodeo, Bolado Park, San Benito (third weekend)
Guadalupana Jamaica Fiesta, San Benito County (third weekend)
Midsummer Music Festival, Sigmund Stern Grove, San Francisco (through August)
Highway 50 Wagon Train, Placerville (or first weekend of July)
Secession Day, Rough and Ready, (June 27)
San Francisco Birthday Celebration

July

San Francisco Pops Concert Season begins

Bach Festival, Sunset Center, Carmel
Ice Follies, Winterland, San Francisco
Asian Festival, Oakland Museum
Hoopa Fourth of July Celebration, Hoopa Reservation
Pony Express Celebration, Pollack Pines (first weekend)
Willits Frontier Days (fourth of July weekend)
Arcata Salmon Festival
Garberville Rodeo (third weekend)
San Mateo County Fair and Floral Fiesta, Fairgrounds
Woodminster Musical Series, Oakland (through September)
Old-Fashioned Fourth, Mt. Shasta
Dune Daze, Samoa
Grand Comedy Festival, Eureka
Old Fashioned 4th of July, Crescent City
Water Carnival, Monte Rio
Jeepers Jamboree, Georgetown to Lake Tahoe
Fiesta-Rodeo de San Juan Bautista (July 16)
Marin Shakespeare Festival (July 15-September)
Captain Weber Days, Stockton (second and third weeks)
OBON Festival, Monterey (second weekend)
Salinas Valley Rodeo (third weekend)
Cooley Junior Rodeo, McCloud
Scotts Valley Days, Scotts Valley (last weekend)
Gold Rush Jubilee, Callahan, Siskiyou County (last weekend)
Feast of Lanterns, Pacific Grove (fourth weekend)
Orick Rodeo
Fortuna Rodeo

August

Old Adobe Days, Petaluma
Monterey County Fair, Fairgrounds
Humboldt County Fair, Ferndale (first weekend)
"Annie & Mary Day", Blue Lake (Aug. 1 and first weekend)
Flea Market, San Juan Bautista
Santa Clara County Fair, San Jose

Ringling Brothers Circus, Oakland
El Dorado Days at Mt. Ranch, San Andreas
Carnival of Gems, Golden Gate Park, San Francisco
Mother Lode Fair, Rodeo, Loggers Contest, Sonora
Plumas County Fair, Quincy (second week)
Pony Express Day, McKinleyville (Aug. 22)
Children's Fairyland Birthday Week, Oakland (last week)
Air Round-Up, Red Bluff (last weekend)
Willow Creek Bigfoot Days

September

Monterey Jazz Festival, Fairgrounds
Renaissance Pleasure Faire & Ha'Penny Market, Marin County (through Oct.)
Mendocino Co. Fair & Apple Show, Boonville
Ringling Brothers Circus, Cow Palace, San Francisco
San Francisco Outdoor Art Festival, Civic Center
Fall Festival, Japantown, San Francisco
San Francisco Opera Season
Berkeley Arts Festival, Civic Center, Provo Park
Antiques Show and Sale, San Francisco
Baccari's Annual Vintage Festival, Hall of Flowers, Golden Gate Park, San Francisco
California State Fair, Sacramento
Scottish Games, Santa Rosa Fairgrounds
Pageant of Fire Mountain, Johnson's Beach, Guerneville (Fri. and Sat. after Labor Day weekend)
Vintage Car Fair, California Nursery, Fremont
American Indian Day, Indian Grinding Rock, Volcano (fourth Friday)
Paul Bunyan Days, Fort Bragg (Labor Day Weekend)
Santa Cruz County Fair, Watsonville
Big Foot Days, Willow Creek,

Humboldt County (Labor Day Weekend)

Redwood Invitational Regatta, Big Lagoon, Humboldt County

Fiesta de San Carlos Borromeo, Carmel

Oktoberfest, San Mateo Fairgrounds

Lodi Grape Festival (second or third weekend)

Fiesta Patrias, Woodland

Castroville Artichoke Festival (second weekend)

Walnut Festival, Walnut Creek (third weekend)

Sonoma Valley of the Moon Festival (last weekend)

October

Laguna Seca Grand Prix, Monterey

Fortuna Arts Festival

Sonoma Co. Harvest Festival Fair, Santa Rosa

National Livestock Exposition, Horse Show and Rodeo, Cow Palace, San Francisco

San Francisco 49ers Football, Candlestick Park (through December)

Pumpkin Pickin, Half Moon Bay

Oakland Raiders, Coliseum (through December)

Spanishtown Art and Pumpkin Festival

Candle Lighter Ghost House, Fremont

Pro-Am Surfing International, West Cliff Drive, Santa Cruz

Blessing of the Fleet, Fisherman's Wharf, San Francisco (first Sunday)

Old Timers' Day, King City

Columbus Day Festival, San Carlos

Columbus Day Celebration, North Beach, San Francisco

Butterfly Parade, Pacific Grove

Reedley Festival

Chinese Double Ten Celebration, San Francisco

San Francisco International Film Festival

Discovery Day, Bodega Bay

November

North California Boat and Sports Show, Coliseum, Oakland

Christmas Balloon Parade, San Jose, (day after Thanksgiving)

December

Christmas Art and Music Festival, Eureka (first weekend)

San Francisco Symphony Season

The Great Dickens Faire & Pickwick Comic Annual, San Francisco

The Nutcracker Ballet, San Francisco

Festival of the Trees, Monterey

Shriners East-West Football Game, Candlestick Park, San Francisco (December 31)

Annual Children's Christmas Pageant, Oakland

Lighting of the Tree of Lebanon, Santa Rosa

Index